## Methuen Playscripts

The Methuen Playscripts series exists to extend the range of plays in print by publishing work which is not yet widely known but which has already earned a place in the acting repertoire of the modern theatre.

## This Jockey Drives Late Nights

Henry Living's latest play takes its story from Leo Tolstoy's The Power of Darkness. As the author has said, it might well have come out of last Sunday's News of the World. The tale of blood and lust it portrays concerns a taxi-hire firm in which the proprietor is murdered by his wife so that she can marry a young man on the staff, only to see him then become embroiled with her own daughter. Presented in a sequence of sparely written narrative scenes, sometimes wrily comic, sometimes shatteringly savage, the action is carried along towards hideous tragedy by powerful songs, and shows Henry Livings in formidable command of his wide-ranging dramatic gifts.

**By the same author**

Good Grief!
The Little Mrs Foster Show
Honour and Offer
Pongo Plays 1-6

# THIS JOCKEY DRIVES LATE NIGHTS

---

HENRY LIVINGS

a play from The Power of Darkness by Leo Tolstoy

First published in Great Britain in 1972
by Eyre Methuen Ltd
11 New Fetter Lane, London EC4P 4EE


Set by Expression Printers Ltd
Printed in Great Britain by
Redwood Press Ltd, Trowbridge, Wiltshire

SBN 413 29480 3 Hardback
413 29490 0 Paperback

This Jockey Drives Late Nights was first presented at The Midlands Arts Centre on Thursday 27 January 1972 with the following cast:

| | |
|---|---|
| THE SINGER | David Francis |
| ANNIE PETERS | Marjorie Yates |
| MILTON PETERS | Tim Stern |
| AGNES PETERS | Carolyn Gilmour |
| MARION PETERS | Rachel Davies |
| DRIVER | Ian Ruskin |
| MR MATHER | Bob Peck |
| MRS MATHER | Sylvia Barter |
| NICK MATHER | Jack Carr |
| MARIE LEES | Miriam Newhouse |
| MICHAEL | John Livesey |
| MR WHITEHEAD | John Dove |
| GUESTS | Clare Blenkinsop |
| | Bill Hartley |
| | Jane Heyman |
| POLICEMAN | David Francis |
| THE GROUP | Paul Clements |
| | John Dove |
| | Bob Peck |
| | Ian Ruskin |
| | assisted by |
| | Michael Brown |

Directed by Philip Hedley
Original music by Alex Glasgow
Designed by Di Seymour
Costumes by Janet Goodwin

## Actors' Note

This play is intended to show people at work, living an ordinary life, in theatrical terms. A great deal of the action takes place against a background of continuing business necessity, or is dictated by business necessity. To save writing 'meanwhile' at intervals through the script I'd like actors to examine the text for their real cues, rather than wait until everyone else has stopped talking.

This applies particularly to Act One, where there is a dialogue written for people taking taxi bookings, which should underlie the domestic dialogue; and to the MARIE/ANNIE row and the ANNIE/NICK/MRS MATHER row, in Act Two scenes one and two respectively: each person is speaking a monologue.

## Act One

Over the stage hangs a large ball covered with small sections of mirror, turning slowly; this accompanies the songs, but remains still during dramatic action. At the back of the stage three doors.

AGNES PETERS, a dense and ugly twenty-five, prepares the stage, as she will do through the play, rearranging furniture, setting props etc. Her task at the moment is to set two brightly lacquered bentwood chairs, a table, and on the table a radio link and bookings ledger, and a coloured telephone. The rest of the stage is bare and scrubbed clean; anything dropped or any dirty marks, AGNES cleans them up.

SINGER enters, once the stage is set and the ball spinning, looking very smart and shiney.

SINGER (sings): Late nights and shaky white days
Ain't drinking takes away my bright eyes
Ain't bad living gives me my grey face

This jockey drives late nights yes sir
This jockey drives late nights
I see a shadow of a running man
On my windshield there's a shadow there
There's a shadow of a running man.

Hire-car jockey goes rocking by
So tired maybe the eight-wheel coach tonight
Cigarettes and diesel rank tea and petrol

This jockey etc...

Oh that tinkling key that jails me
Takes away my days stoned out
Cat's eyes snake on... sparks-from-the-big-knife-grinder

This jockey etc...

Man at the wheel says nothing
Locked up in thunder this man
Clock don't go from way back, gave up

This jockey etc...

Two matchsticks hold my lids up

Boys like the mouse in the wheel he says
One day I'll reach the end of this long journey

This jockey etc...

MILTON PETERS, a prematurely aged sixty-five, weak from a lifetime of broken nights, an undermined constitution, enters applauding the number. The effort of standing and clapping at the same time becomes too much, and he folds feebly onto one of the chairs, allowing him to re-allocate enough energy for a couple of hearty claps as the SINGER goes off.

MILTON: 'Kyou. Very nice.

The telephone starts to ring, interrupting MILTON's intention to introduce himself to us.

MILTON: Isn't it marvellous how you can't hear a blind thing when a phone's ringing? I say isn't it marvellous how you can't hear a...

ANNIE PETERS, MILTON's wife, enters; forty-five, brisk, smart, handsome.

MILTON:..Somebody answer that phone.

ANNIE does so.

MILTON: Can't hear a thing with that ringing.

ANNIE (to MILTON): You what?

MILTON, however, can now introduce himself.

MILTON: Milton Peters. Peters' Taxis.

ANNIE (on phone): Peters' Taxis..Yes. Right.

MILTON: Wife and daughter: Annie and Agnes; about as much use as athlete's foot, the pair of 'em.

The phone starts ringing again, as ANNIE leaves it to go to the radio link.

MILTON: Agnes! the phone!

ANNIE (on radio link): Party at Jackson Road. Four. Now.

The radio gives out a burping gargle of a reply.

ANNIE: Thank you yes, the Falcon... thank you Yellow three.

MILTON: Can't you hear that phone? It's ringing dammit. Agnes! (Calls:) Nick!

ANNIE (on radio link): The Arden Club, Arden Road. Anybody take Arden Road, within half an hour?

MILTON: Nick!

AGNES: What is it Dad?

MILTON: Can't you hear me shouting?

AGNES: Yes.

NICK, an overly handsome twenty; looks good in his clean shirt and neat tie, which is all you can see of his driver's livery as he now has overalls on; his hands are black with grease, as he shows MILTON.

NICK: Look, I'll come when I have time.

MILTON: Answer that phone will you Nick lad? (To us, indicating NICK:) Nick Mather: hired man. (Wheezes his way through an incapacitating cough.) Every picture tells a story.

NICK: You can see the state I'm in. I'm fully occupied.

Phone stops.

NICK: Anyway, what phone?

MILTON: Look, if you've got something to do, kindly get about it.

NICK goes. Phone starts up again.

MILTON: Nick! come and see to this phone! Agnes phone!

AGNES: Have I to answer it? (She answers it.)

MILTON (to us): She's having the operation. . they want to find out if there's any work left in her.

ANNIE (on the radio link): Yellow two? Thank you, right away, good. Arden Club, Arden Road. They're ready now, any time. Drop at the Airport.

MILTON: Did you hear the way he spoke to me? He's idle; he's been messing with that choke since ten tonight. If I had my health I wouldn't keep him another minute; I'd be better off with a partner; someone with a reason for working.

AGNES (meanwhile, on the phone): Manchester Street, yes. Where are you? Crowsford? Crowsford Station, thank you. Soon as we've got a car.

ANNIE (to MILTON): You're not so damn brisk yourself; you'll get as far as the back kitchen and back in here to your chair and that's about it. (To AGNES:) Where for love? (To MILTON again:) Nattering other people's about all you've strength for.

MILTON: Olympic long jump, Berlin, 1936.

ANNIE: You what?

MILTON drums two fingers on his chair with an accelerating rhythm until he takes off in the 'jump'.. fully four seconds airborne, lands.

MILTON: Tumultuous applause.

After a moment, ANNIE is able to drag her attention back to AGNES from this specimen she somehow married.

AGNES: Want picking up at Crowsford Station as soon as possible mother, for Manchester Street, I think he said.

ANNIE (on the radio link): Anybody take Crowsford Station?

MILTON: I supply the brains, and the imagination.

The radio belches out a response, which ANNIE seems to understand.

ANNIE: Crowsford Station, yes. Thank you Yellow five.

MILTON: Where is he now?

AGNES: Who?

MILTON: Nick. Where is he?

AGNES: Outside.

MILTON: I bloody know he's outside; he's not in here is he? What's he doing I mean.

AGNES: Eh? He's talking with someone that's all.

The phone rings. ANNIE answers it.

MILTON: I shouldn't pay him in washers for what he does; do I pay him for talking? Who's he talking with?

AGNES: You what?

ANNIE (meanwhile on the phone): Alpine Social Club, right. Yes, right, as soon as possible.

MARION, daughter of MILTON and ANNIE, twenty-one, bright,

but tired now, comes in from outside. She has smart slacks and a blazer, long hair. Car keys in her hand.

MARION: Anything just now?

ANNIE: Alpine Social Club just Marion love.

MILTON (to us): That's my youngest. And hers. Marion.

MARION: Right. Nick's Mum and Dad've just got off the bus. He's to go home and get wed.

ANNIE (looks up sharply, then back at the ledger): You're a bloody liar.

MARION: That's what he says. He's just shouted me as I was coming in: 'Come to my wedding', he says. He was laughing. Says he's packing in here. (Going.) Alpine Social Club.

ANNIE (calls after her): Name's Bennett! (To MILTON:) Well, you heard? He's off.

MILTON: Who? Nick?

ANNIE: Yes, bloody Nick.

MILTON: There's no need for bloody swearing. Anyway there's plenty more'n him and better. I didn't know he was courting.

ANNIE: He's subbed more'n a months wages off you; you're aware of that?

MILTON: He can work that off when I've got summer trips to do..

ANNIE: Oh aye, you're glad enough for him to go, and save his wages in the winter.

MILTON: I just pay him overtime, if he earns it; his eight hours are mine d'you see? Works out quite well..

ANNIE: Me and Marion'll have it all to do, I know; and you festering in here the while.

MILTON: I'm not healthy.

ANNIE: You've two coaches out in all weathers because you won't pay for a garage; that banger that he's working on that you should have traded in this many a long month..

MILTON holds out a hand to her, palm up.

MILTON: High jump. (His eyes follow the rise of an imaginary jumper up and then down to the ground, where he stamps his foot on the tiny athlete.) Antwerp 1920.

AGNES (gathering her wits): Not a day passes without something falling off one or other of the motors, and you want to get shut of the only decent mechanic you've got. You don't think I'm going to do it all do you? I'll tell you what I'll do, I'll sit down next to you!

The phone starts up again.

ANNIE: You can suit yourself, I'm not going to do a man's work!

MILTON: Agnes, can you not hear that phone? Answer it.

AGNES: What? the phone? (She answers it.)

ANNIE: You can sit here and take the calls, I won't! you clean the cars and keep them going. You do something for a change!

MILTON: Honestly it's like trying to live in a revolving door; have you suddenly gone daft or was it gradual? (Shuffles off towards the street.)

ANNIE: You're useless for work and you're useless for the other; all you're fit for is eating sandwiches on the lavatory and reading the bloody almanac!

MILTON: I'll be outside if you want me. (Exit.)

ANNIE (screams after him): Forty minutes you had in there this morning you miserable mouldy-rotten warmed-up corpse! Want you? Who the bloody hell'd want you and what for?

MILTON reappears briefly.

MILTON: There's no need for language Annie my angel.

ANNIE gives a snarl of rage and frustration.

MILTON disappears.

AGNES (she's jotted the phone message down and hands it to ANNIE): What you yelling at Dad for?

ANNIE: And you can bloody keep out of it an all.

AGNES: I know, and don't think I don't. It's you that's miserable mouldy rotten, Dad hasn't done nothing. It's you.

ANNIE: Talk about something you understand, and keep out of

this, I warned you. (Sudden snap. ) And put that flaming broom down and find something useful to do blast you.

AGNES slams out of the room taking the broom with her.

AGNES (off): Bitch! bloody damn bitch! We've all had enough of you you know that?

ANNIE, alone, gives way to her distress, unable to speak to us for a moment. Finally, hammering out the word, hoping to empty it of the meaning it obviously has:

ANNIE: Marry. Marry. Marry marry marry marry. He _can't_.

ANNIE waits, mouth half-open, for the pain to drain through her.

ANNIE: Ouf... that hurts.. That does hurt.

NICK enters, cleaned up, a bit assertive in his uncertainty.

NICK: Hallo darling. Look, don't say anything just yet, but my Mum and Dad are here, and they want me home with them. I know it sounds silly, but there's this girl over our way, and anyway my Dad reckons I ought to marry her. I know it sounds queer, but there it is.

ANNIE: Well you go then, and get married; you've obviously made up your mind.

NICK: Be sensible Annie, we can discuss it can't we? All you say is away and get married; what's up?

ANNIE (gasps): What's up? What's up? You ask me some very funny questions you do. Go on, if you're going. Get out!

NICK: Stop it Annie, did I say I wanted to go? It's not that I _want_ to go; now be honest, did I say that? What I was thinking was, why don't I go and do as they say, marry, and then come back here? To you I mean. Just because I'm married at home doesn't say I have to live at home does it?

ANNIE: Don't you dare talk to me like that; it's not enough you go tampering with some little scrubber, you have to go marrying with her next. How d'you think I feel? Eh? D'you think I want you, stinking from her bed, alternate bloody Mondays?

NICK: Annie, that's filthy talk; I don't want to hear it.

ANNIE: Get out of my sight, just don't talk to me.

NICK: Oh Annie, I wish you'd be sensible. What can I do? I can't go against what my Dad says now can I?

ANNIE: Oh yes, it's your father that's doing it is it? I bet. You've been messing about with that Marie all this time, and she's coming the old soldier now, I know; got fed-up of working for wages and thinks she's got a feller nailed at long last. Now I know what she was up to coming here the other day. I was wondering about that; it's a long trip for just saying hallo.

NICK: Annie, Annie, I wish you'd just be sensible; it's calf love; she just hangs round me, I can't help that now can I? I'm away from you when I go home on my days off, and I'm bound to be vunerable aren't I? I mean you know that.

ANNIE: So what's your father doing here then? How does he get into the act? You bloody put him up to it because you hadn't the guts to make your own decisions, you a bloody grown man.. (At last she bursts into angry wild tears.)

NICK: I can't understand why you don't believe me what I say: nobody put anybody up to anything: it's my Dad's own idea entirely, Marie must have talked to him.

ANNIE: If it's not your idea, if you're against it, how come you're falling in with it?

NICK: Look, understand me Annie, I don't want to marry; but how can I possibly go against what my Dad says? What possible argument have I got?

ANNIE: Just tell them no!

NICK: Ah now Annie, be sensible; it's not as easy as that. I'd have to say why; surely you can see that?

ANNIE (if he says the word 'sensible' once more, she may go mad): If you marry with her, Nick I don't honestly know what I'll do. I'll kill myself. I've done wrong, I know that, and stupid too, but there's no helping that. Everything in me cries out for you, and if you go, I'll do away with myself, because I shan't have any alternative. D'you understand me Nick? No alternative whatever. No chance, from here on.

NICK: I don't want to go away, I told you that; I wish you'd listen to what I say Annie; you'll have me crying next. If I'd wanted to go I could have gone long since. Scott's was offering me a manager's job, but I didn't, I reckoned to stay where I was wanted. I mean if you don't want me here thing's'll be different.

ANNIE (just under control): Nick, just think the old man can't live so long; then we'll have a chance to put things right. I could wed you Nick, if you'd a mind. This place could be yours.

NICK: No, now no, I don't want to hear you talk that way Annie; I've no ambitions in that direction so don't go thinking I have Annie; it's up to us to be sensible. Just don't blame me, because certain women fancy me, that's all.

ANNIE covers her hurt mouth with her hand, so that only a whimper escapes as she considers this block she dotes on.

ANNIE: Will you still love me? Or not?

NICK (goes to her): Come here and I'll show you. (Takes her in his arms. ) I couldn't ever forget you my darling.

They fold into each other's arms, and kiss.

MRS MATHER, NICK's mother, comes in.

MRS MATHER (to us): My name's Mrs Mather. (Indicates NICK without herself looking:) Nicholas's mother. (She continues to gaze, earnestly and discreetly at us. )

The phone rings.

ANNIE and NICK spring apart. They see MRS MATHER, still earnestly gazing at us. ANNIE answers the phone.

ANNIE (on the phone): Peters' Taxis. . Yes. . Arenton Road. . yes. (She drags the ledger towards her. ) I've nothing here at the moment. . twenty minutes. . yes. Thank you. Twenty minutes. (She goes to the radio link and asks for a car to take this booking. ) Arenton Road in twenty minutes anybody? Arenton Road, twenty minutes.

The radio burps out its response.

ANNIE: Party of two twenty minutes. Yes. Thank you.

MRS MATHER and NICK speak quietly and privately.

MRS MATHER: Now then Nicholas darling: your father and me was wondering where you was; going off like that.

NICK: I was in here.

MRS MATHER: That's right, you was wan't you – Only I didn't see you for a minute when I come in; the phone was as much a surprise to me as it was to you. Go on with you now while me and Mrs Peters has a word, and bless you. And just one word in your ear: you're young once Nicholas darling, once only; enjoy yourself while you've the chance: it doesn't come twice. Go on I say, Mr Peters is asking after you outside.

NICK: Wherever he is he's asking after me; I only came in to tell her the car was ready.

MRS MATHER: Mm. I know who's ready and what for. (Nudges him rosily.) Bless you lad.

NICK: Mum, it's very embarrassing Dad and you coming like this; I mean he's no need to come talking to Mr Peters like this, what's it to do with him? And telling the world I've got to get married; it's not very modern is it?

MRS MATHER: Get on with you I said; it's all a notion of your Dad's; you know what a budgie he is; I don't think he's heard Mafeking's been relieved either. I just want a word here with Mrs Peters, so away with you.

NICK: It's just that it's very embarrassing, I mean I don't want to have to insult Dad or anything, but what does he think he'll gain? I'm a grown man you know mother. (Goes on his way.)

MRS MATHER: Exactly Nicholas.

NICK: I'm going to have it out you know: get things straight with him before things get out of hand: a man has a right to have his say. (Exit.)

MRS MATHER: Evening darling. How are you?

ANNIE smiles wanly.

MRS MATHER: I thought your Milton looked a mite pale.

ANNIE: Oh yes?

MRS MATHER: Yes.

ANNIE: You've come to fetch Nick home seemingly.

MRS MATHER: Whoever said that?

ANNIE: Marion came in saying he's to go home and get married; it's all a bit sudden isn't it?

MRS MATHER: What'd he live off at our house darling? Eh? We've no money to help him, the shop brings in nothing. There's no work round our way darling, no work. Besides he's getting on well here isn't he? Eh? You're not wanting to get rid of him are you? I thought you were suited with him.

ANNIE: You saw.

MRS MATHER: What's that darling?

ANNIE: I daresay it's wrong, what's between me and your Nick, but I love him, he makes me happy, and I can't help myself.

MRS MATHER: There now, fancy. We can't help ourselves, us women can we? Anyway as I was saying, your Milton looks very pale.

ANNIE: Oh?

MRS MATHER: Here's something that might help. (She hoists out a pharmaceutical jar from her capacious handbag.) You try these on him. Now it's all right, they're just pills to pep him up. You see if he doesn't take to them. Take to them. Poor sort of a night isn't it? Just a minute ago I was saying to my Nicholas I said you don't get chances twice, I said. Anyway what was I saying? Oh yes, your Milton. He's no strength left has he? He's bloodless. All those late nights; that's not where you get your rest, in a chair, you have to sleep, in a bed. Nothing to him, shot. Yes, I said, Nicholas darling, you're only young once I said.

ANNIE: Just so he won't leave us.

MRS MATHER: Nor will he darling; it's him, Mr Mather; you know what he's like, the old barmpot. He gets some notion in his head and nothing'll dislodge it. Eh dearie me it's a smile for sure.

ANNIE: How did it start?

MRS MATHER: Well darling, you know how Nicholas was working on the railway at that time? Yes, well there was this lass in the canteen. Orphan she is.

ANNIE: Marie Lees.

MRS MATHER: That's right, Marie Lees, funny you should know her. Now it's not for me to say, whether Nicholas and her had relations or not; he's a young man and no denying it; you could imagine; but whether or not, Mr Mather heard there was.

ANNIE: There was what?

MRS MATHER: Something. Either he heard it from others or else she come along and told him herself some time; anyway there it is he's convinced of it.

ANNIE (low voice): Oh my God.

MRS MATHER: And you know him: bonehead that he is, he gets it into his head we've to come here and tell Nicholas he's to do the right thing. I expect he's been talking in the taproom and he daren't face them without he's done something; you know they get themselves in a corner and can't get out. I couldn't say anthing that'd in-sense him. Righto I says to myself, if that's how it is, I'll come another way about it. They're obstinate, you know; just one idea in their heads, so how's the old fool to know I'm not harbouring a hundred different eh? That's how you go about it with men darling.

ANNIE: She came here after him; I realize it now. Marie Lees. Then when he said just now to Marion that he was going away and he was going to marry, I knew. It was like a knife through me; I was convinced that was what he wanted. Suddenly it all turns round, and what you thought before becomes the opposite, the complete opposite. I didn't consider it before, but somewhere I was convinced he wouldn't ever go away, and that made it all all right; then suddenly, upside down. I can't live through it if he goes away. Not ever I didn't think he'd go away.

MRS MATHER: Now you're not to talk like that darling. Anyway where was I? Oh yes, your Milton.

ANNIE: Take my word for it I'm sick and tired of the sight of him.

MRS MATHER: Yes, that's how it goes. Oh, I was nearly forgetting these (the pills). It's this feller in our road, works nights. He says on no account take more than six in a day, not more than six. You may think you're all right, but anybody that's a bit weak constitutionally could kill himself taking more than six; there was a lass got addicted and brought herself to starvation; took away her appetite for food completely.

ANNIE: Now then Mrs Mather, be careful what you say.

MRS MATHER: How d'you mean? Have I said anything?

ANNIE: He has some pills already, from the doctor. Coloured, like those. They help him to keep awake, with him having to be up most nights.

MRS MATHER: There you are then, that's it isn't it? I had a notion you'd find a use for them. I gave thirty bob.

ANNIE: Supposing something goes wrong?

MRS MATHER: I should be interested to know what's wrong with giving a man some pills which he has already from his own accredited doctor; anyway I don't know what it's got to do with me; suit yourself, it's entirely up to you.

ANNIE: My head's splitting. I'm afraid. Afraid of what might happen.

MRS MATHER: Well I don't know I'm sure; I came here to be helpful; I can just as easily take them back with me; some folks'd be glad of a lift.

ANNIE: He just swallows the others, I've seen him.

MRS MATHER: Same with these, no need for a drink, and they've no taste; he'll take to them, you see; he'll think he's getting his health back; it'll please him. You're going to be sensible are you or not?

ANNIE (takes the pill jar at last): I'd never have entertained the thought if it weren't all such a mess; I've got this dreadful headache I don't know where from.

MRS MATHER: What's that darling? Thirty shillings I paid; you'll not forget that? Had to take it out of the rent money see.

ANNIE: Yes, yes. I was forgetting. (Gets the money out of a small petty cash box and pays MRS MATHER.)

MRS MATHER: He'll be grateful, except that he won't know, not if you've any sense he won't know. You just keep topping up his supply, so't he's got some when he wants 'em. Nobody'll ask; if they do, who's to know he didn't buy them for himself?
See now here's Mr Peters and my husband. (To us:) Mr Mather.

The radio gives a garbled gurgle, and ANNIE goes to answer it.

MILTON creeps in, followed by MR MATHER, a caricatured version of his son; manly and righteous, a pipe between his nervously grinning dentures, rosy and feverishly energetic.

ANNIE (on the radio link): No, nothing just now, you can come in.

The radio gurgles.

ANNIE: All right, yes.

MATHER: I want to have things right you see Mr Peters, that's what it is, yes. My idea was for Nick to come home and work in the shop, see. We've got his room still.

MILTON: Yes, yes, all right, I expect you would have; unless of course you've had some more babies in the meantime..

MRS MATHER: Oops, Mr Peters!

MATHER: Eh, what's that? (To MRS MATHER:) What did he say?

MILTON: Oh sit down for heaven's sake. We can have a talk about it can't we?

MATHER: What?

MILTON: Has Nick got an idea to marry, is that what it is?

MRS MATHER: Has he buggery Mr Peters. It's him (her husband); I don't know what he's on about; you know yourself how we're fixed, and there's little enough room in the house..

MATHER: There's his room still..

MRS MATHER: I bloody know there's his room still. (To MILTON again:) I mean, Mr Peters, where would he live, with a family? If a family was to start?

MILTON: Quite.

MRS MATHER: I mean it's not as if there was some sort of rush on; it's not a rush job if you know what I mean.

MILTON: Will one of you explain or not? Nick's thinking of marrying.

MRS MATHER: Yes, only he's not, so far as I know.

MILTON: Eh?

MATHER: I have this job in town now you see, and that brings us in a bit more..

MRS MATHER: Job he calls it! Lavatory attendant!

MATHER: Well what's wrong with that then?

MRS MATHER: He came home the other night and he had me puking.

MILTON: Oh bloody Norah..

MATHER: It's mostly the carbolic. It takes your breath away at first, granted; but you get accustomed, and truth to tell it's no worse than the brewery when the wind's that way (to her) and we've always had that. I change the minute I get in. So anyway, Nick could look after the shop, and I'd be bringing in a bit..

MILTON: You want Nick to see to the shop now?

MATHER: Er, yes, I think so, yes.

MILTON: Fair enough, I get it. He's subbed over a month's wages you know that, because it was for your bills he did it.

MATHER: Ah, yes, I know I know. Once you get behind with the wholesalers' accounts you can't call your soul your own. Nick'll stick by his bargain, and so shall we, don't think we won't. Yes I see; well, I wonder could you see your way for him to have a bit of time off, I mean with him getting married.

ANNIE: There's not much work coming in, could you see to the taxis for a while Milton..?

MRS MATHER: You should be here for this Annie love...

ANNIE: Well I shan't be..

MILTON: Oh sit down and shut your gob woman. Now, Nick's definitely married then is he? (To ANNIE:) Now where're you going?

ANNIE: Out. (Goes.)

MILTON: Oh stay where you are: suppose the phone rings?

MRS MATHER: It fascinates me, it really does, I mean, here we all sit, nodding our heads and agreeing about it all. I mean is Nick to be consulted or not? Mr Peters, I just wish you knew who it is he's proposing our Nicholas should marry that's all; she's a slag I'm not kidding.

MATHER: Not a bit of it no! you've no reason whatever to say that of her; Nick's entirely in the wrong.

MRS MATHER: Much you know.

MILTON: How's he in the wrong?

MATHER: Nick did wrong by her, you see.

MRS MATHER: Oh shut up and I'll tell him; Mr Peters, you know he used to work for the railway before he came to you? He had a mechanical horse you know, mm. Now there's this girl in the canteen, Marie Lees, a bit simple she is. Anyway she's been round at our house, asking after him. And that's about the price of it. He reckons she's told him our Nicholas. . you know, seduced her. Promised her and now he's chucked her.

MILTON: And has he?

MRS MATHER: She can't have so much pride whether or not can she? And she's anybody's.

MATHER: Now you've no business saying that and I don't know why you do. .

MRS MATHER: Because I've some bloody respect for my own bloody son that's why! Mr Peters, ask about after this girl, everybody'll tell you the same, she's a scrubber. Known for it.

MILTON: If that's how it is Albert, he'd be lumbered wouldn't he?

MATHER (to MRS MATHER): I don't know how you can stand there and lie to me! Why? What's got into you? She's a good girl. And I'm right sorry for her if she's to be left.

MRS MATHER: Hark at him! he's sorry for her! What about our Nicholas if you want anybody to be sorry for? She'll do nothing but drag him back, and you know it, a millstone; you talk bloody rubbish you do that.

MATHER: It is not rubbish!

MRS MATHER: Don't interrupt me you! I haven't finished talking yet!

MATHER: I say it isn't rubbish! You twist everything to suit your own book; I don't know what you're up to but what's wrong's wrong and you won't talk it right, and if he doesn't pay for it, we shall.

MRS MATHER: Ooh you make me tired talking to you.

MATHER: She's a clean, decent, hard-working girl; she didn't start off with so many chances, and she's asked for nothing from anyone; and the first one she gives her trust to lets her down..

MRS MATHER: That's what they all say.

MATHER: What they all say? Is that what you said?

MRS MATHER: Don't you dare..

MATHER: Is that what you said when I stuck by you? What sort of a man would you have thought me to be if I'd walked out on you when..

MRS MATHER: Shurrup!!! Don't you bloody compare me with that slag!

MATHER: What I want to know is is Marie Lees a human being or isn't she? Are we God's children or not? What would you do if you was tret like Marie Lees is?

MRS MATHER: He just goes on and bloody on, I could murder him..

MILTON: Albert, you don't have to believe everything a young girl says now do you? And don't you think Nick should be consulted about who he's going to marry? If he's made a promise, he'll stand by it. Annie, away and fetch him in; he's not a liar Albert.

ANNIE goes outside as told.

MRS MATHER: Thank goodness somebody's talking sensible at last; you can't be forced into marriage these days you silly old goat; his feelings have to be studied you know. He'll tell you get stuffed, and quite right too; he's just nicely settled here, why should he shift for you? Summer trips coming along, plenty of overtime and gratuities... oh yes, I was going to ask you to give us a bit of a lift Mr Peters, on account, you know how things are...

MATHER: It catches up with you, you see, you make a rod for your own back...

MRS MATHER: His Master's Voice. He's like a budgie I swear..

MATHER: If you've got a clear conscience, if you've got Christian teaching you can go your way light-hearted. That's how it seems to me anyway.

MRS MATHER: Yes, all right, you know best love..

MATHER: It finds you out you know. Only this last winter these three lads round our way..

MRS MATHER makes a winding motion with her hand, as if her husband were a clockwork gramophone. MILTON has a matchbox between his index and little fingers on the table top.

MATHER: .. they borrowed this wagon, and they were seen loading coal at this yard, that wasn't theirs you see; one of them worked there.. you don't get away with these things you see.

MILTON raises the matchbox from the table top by straightening his two middle fingers.

The others are attracted by his absorption.

He looks up at them furtively. Nods down to his hand to indicate the feat.

MILTON: The clean and jerk: Arkadiy Vorbobyev: Olympic Middle-heavyweight Champion: 1956 and 1960.

NICK enters this area of tranced silence: three people considering a matchbox that isn't doing anything.

NICK (after a moment): Somebody want me?

MARION follows NICK in and goes to check jobs at the ledger.

MILTON: Sit you down a minute Nick.

NICK surveys the occupied chairs of the room.

NICK: I'm as well standing.

MILTON: Your mother and father and me have been talking.

NICK: Well you'd no business to had you?

MILTON: Not if you was in the right, I suppose not. I see you know what we were discussing.

NICK: It's obvious. And whether I was in the right or the wrong you'd still no business to.

MATHER: Now you just listen, I'm talking now and I want answers you cheeky young monkey.

NICK: Oh Norah, listen to him will you. .

MATHER: Did you or did you not promise this girl?

NICK: I don't know what you're talking about.

MATHER: Did you or did you not promise this girl? Did you take advantage of her innocence? Did you promise her and seduce her and all that?

NICK: Oh honestly Dad you talk like a Victorian novel. .

MATHER: Did you or did you not? Did you talk marriage to her in any way?

MILTON: Can you not give a straight answer to your father's question Nick?

NICK: I've never heard of such a daft situation, I mean times have changed you know. .

MATHER: You can cover up in front of others now Nick, but if you've done wrong it'll find you out, be warned; tne straight truth now. She's no family to turn to, so it's easy enough to make light of her; times may have changed, but people haven't; people have to be respected; you tell me how it was between you.

NICK: I'd be interested to know who you think you're talking to. Look: there's nothing to tell, barring what I've told you already outside. I knew her, in the canteen, I knew who she was. Marie Lees. Finish. Of course if you listen to her sooner than your own son that's up to you, it's no odds to me; I can't stop her saying what she's a mind to. How about her and Fred Maxton besides?

MATHER: Nick, listen, think on what you're saying, a lie'll find you out: was there anything or not? Did you have carnal knowledge of Marie Lees on the pretext you'd promised her marriage?

MRS MATHER: Thinks he's in the Old Bailey I swear to God.

MATHER: Have you got the courage to answer my questions Nick?

NICK: Oh my God doesn't he go <u>on</u>; look I <u>told</u> you, there was nothing between us, word of honour; I know nothing bar what I said.

Pause.

NICK: And I must say I admire your nerve the way you talk to me. The lot of you. It's fantastic.

MRS MATHER (referring to her husband): What a dunderhead. (To him directly:) You have to go believing every word anyone tells you don't you? It's pathetic.

MATHER: I'm not ashamed.

MRS MATHER (to NICK): You've got a good boss Nicholas, and you stick to him. I've had a word over your summer overtime. . he's agreeable.

MILTON: Are we finished with it now then?

MATHER: Think on Nick, if you're breaking a promise given it'll catch up with you: I know life.

NICK: Oh balls, I've nothing to reproach myself with; I don't know why you can't all just shut up.

MARION runs out briskly.

MARION: I'll just go and get Mum.

MILTON: What's up? Can't she get herself?

But MARION has gone.

MRS MATHER: He's a riot my Albert, honest; once he's got something into his head, it takes some driving out.

MILTON (his eye on MATHER): Are we finished with it now then?

MATHER: I wasn't for forcing the lad to anything you understand, all I wanted to know was am I wrong, just wanted to get things straight you see. .

MILTON: I'll go so far as to say this Albert: if he's to go away from here now with the summer coming when I've got all the work on, I certainly shan't want him in the winter when I'm scratching for jobs. Full time or nowt. . he's no use to me just when I'm slack. Nick? You're stopping?

NICK: Of course; I wasn't aware that I was going.

MATHER: That's it then; I shall just have to live with it.

MRS MATHER (mutters, attempting good humour for the rest of the room): My sainted aunts will you give over nagging at it? You get on my wick, and everybody else's too I'm sure. (To MILTON:) It's not that we're especially short; but I'm glad I've had a chance to talk with you Mr Peters, Nick doesn't always <u>think</u> you know. . though of course he's the best of lads once it's pointed out to him. .

ANNIE comes in and stands looking round at the others.

MILTON (in evasive reply to MRS MATHER): Yes, well any-way, the Club'll be open just. Agnes! Albert, come and have a drink and then I'll get you run home. Agnes! We're off to the Club!

MATHER: I'm not a drinker.

MILTON: Well you'll have something, and the girls can come too. Come on then.

AGNES appears at the house door.

AGNES: What is it Dad?

MILTON: Eh?

AGNES: Did you shout me?

MILTON: Yes.

MILTON creeps out, followed by MATHER and MRS MATHER and then AGNES.

MILTON: Come on with you Annie; Nick can take any calls that come on.

ANNIE follows, leaving NICK alone. He checks the work ledger.

NICK (to us): Fantastic: on and on. I was shaking, physically shaking, couldn't stop myself. How could I possibly tell the truth to him? 'Yes your honour, I have made love to this woman, I cannot tell a lie.' He gets it all completely wrong, I've never heard such nonsense as he talks. You can't marry every lass you make love to, it's ridiculous.

MARION returns and hurries across the stage.

NICK: Alone at last.

MARION: You what? Dad's forgotten his coat and it's getting cold out.

NICK: So you said, I'll get it Dad, it'll give me a chance for a glance at Nick Mather.

MARION: Ooh, Lochinvar.

AGNES comes in.

AGNES hurries conspiratorially across to NICK.

AGNES: Hey Nick you'd better get out there, there's somebody asking after you. There is honest.

MARION: Who is it? Can't they come in here?

AGNES: It's that Marie Lees that was here before. The one you used to take out when you were working at the Railways. She's waiting just round the corner.

NICK: Is she?

AGNES: Honest.

NICK: What does she want?

AGNES: How do I know? She says you've to come to speak to her. Just wants a word with you she says; I said what about, but she wouldn't tell me. So I said come into the office and she says no. She says is that right you're jacking in with us and I said no; your father'd wanted you to but you weren't going to after all. She says for God's sake make him come out here, I've got to have a word with him. She's been waiting hours it seems; why don't you go?

NICK: Why the hell should I go out there?

AGNES: She says she doesn't want to talk to you in front of everybody, but if necessary she will.

NICK: Take no notice, she'll go away after a bit.

AGNES: She says was it right you were going to marry Marion. Where she get that from.

MARION: Who marry who?

AGNES: Nick and you; she must have got it from somewhere.

MARION: Well I never; I wonder who says that?

NICK: People are talking Marion, we shall have to get wed eh?

MARION: I might have done once over.

NICK: Oh? What's changed?

MARION: You wouldn't love me.

NICK: How's that? I might.

MARION: You've been told not to.

NICK: Who says not?

MARION: My Mum. She might not have said it in so many words, but you've heard her if we spend too much time in your company. And she never takes her eyes off you if you're about.

NICK (laughs uneasily): You've been watching what goes off have you? Crafty.

MARION: I don't have to be so damn crafty to hear the way she went off when I said you were off home to get wed earlier on. Bloody old cow she is. (She goes off into the house.)

AGNES: I'm supposed to be with the others at the Club, they'll be wondering what's happened to me.

AGNES goes out to the street as MARIE comes in. They are strangers more or less, and merely nod as they cross. MARIE stands for a moment, looking at NICK.

MARIE: Nick, what's your idea with me?

NICK: Me? I've no ideas with you.

MARIE: You're just leaving me.

NICK: You're doing yourself no good coming here! Nor me; how d'you mean leaving you? When was I ever with you?

MARIE: Oh Nicky..

NICK: Hell and damn it you're a very strange woman.. whatever did you have to come here for? Hanging round the corner, sending Agnes back in here after me. I didn't come when you knew I knew you were there; so you should have known I didn't want any part of you. Now get off with you and be sensible.

MARIE: You don't want any part of me, that's how we're talking now is it? You made me think different. You've had your fun eh?

NICK: Oh change the record; I've been getting all this from my father; talking to my father, that's what did it for you: that was the last straw. Now just be sensible and scram.

MARIE: Didn't you love me? Didn't you ever love me? What did I do? I can't understand, you said if I loved you I'd go with you and then when I do, and then when I do.. what did I do?

NICK: There's no point dragging it all out like this, get off with you; by God some women are foolish.

MARIE: Nick, I've got no one belonging me, no one. I can stand broken promises; it doesn't hurt that you talked marriage and now won't have it..

NICK: That's a downright lie..

MARIE: You did you did Nick, I promise you. But what hurts bad is that you don't love me any more, I've no one belonging me d'you see? There's no one else at all. And you going with someone else, when you could have had me. What did I ever do?

The phone starts ringing.

NICK: I'd be wasting my breath trying to talk sense into you; get off now, before worse happens, I might forget myself.

MARIE: Worse? Go on, thump me? Go on then why don't you? Oh Nick at least look at me, don't turn your head away.

NICK: Supposing someone was to come in now? I don't know why you keep staying here, it won't make a ha'porth of difference.

The phone gives up.

MARIE: This is it then is it? Is that all there is? It's the end? Finish? I've to forget? I've nobody to turn to, you know that, and you've had no mercy for me. I've nothing now, I might as well be dead. God forgive you for what you've done; God forgive you for making me happy and then taking it away; it's the worst thing you could possibly have done. If you find somebody better you'll forget me, if she's worse you'll think of me. You will think of me then Nicky? (Reaches out to take his head in her hands, whimpering.) I loved you so much and tried to please you. 'Bye Nicky.

NICK (trying to avoid her touch): Now you're just pestering me; if you won't go away I shall have to.

MARIE: Nicky you aren't half a rat.

The phone starts to ring.

MARIE: Don't you understand what I say? I've nobody belonging me? (Running out.) One day you'll go through what I'm going through, though I'm sure I don't hope it for you.

MARION comes out, carrying her father's old top coat. Stands looking at NICK.

NICK (answers the phone): Peters' Taxis. Yes. Yes. Right. I'll book it down. Midnight, yes. The Wagonette, party of two. That'll be all right. (Rings off. Books the job in the ledger.)

MARION: You louse.

NICK: What am I supposed to have done now?

MARION (in tears): It was awful the way she cried. Awful.

NICK: What's up with you?

MARION: What? You did the dirt on her, that's what you did, and you'll play the same trick with me! (She hurries out.)

NICK (to us): That's three of 'em in under a hour; I must be a fantastic feller. Women; they should be put in a hole in the ground and only brought out twice a year: once for treading and once for making tatie pie. (Exit.)

The mirrored ball begins to turn, and the SINGER advances to tell us, with the assistance of an INTERLOCUTOR:

| SINGER (sings): | INTERLOCUTOR (speaks): |
|---|---|
| A la claire fontaine<br>M'en allant promener<br>J'ai trouvé l'eau si pure<br>Que je m'y suis baigné | At the fresh-water pool<br>Where I went walking<br>I found the water so pure<br>That I plunged in |
| Il y a longtemps que je t'aime<br>Jamais je ne t'oublierai | I loved you a long time<br>Never never forget you |
| J'ai trouvé l'eau si belle | I found the water there so lovely |
| Que je m'y suis baigné<br>Sous les feuilles d'un chêne<br>Je me suis fait sêcher | That I bathed there<br>Under an oak tree's leaves<br>I dried myself |
| Il y a longtemps etc | |
| Sur la plus haute branche<br>Un rossignol chantait<br>Rossignol toi qui chante<br>Toi, tu as le coeur gai | Up on the highest branch<br>Sang a nightingale<br>Nightingale, you who sing<br>Your heart is gay |
| Il y a longtemps etc | |
| Tu as le coeur à rire | You have the heart to laugh |

Moi je l'ai-t-à pleurer
J'ai perdu ma maîtresse
Sans l'avoir mérité

Mine is for crying
I have lost my love
For nothing that I did

Il y a longtemps etc

Je voudrais que la rose
Fut encore au rosier
Et moi et ma maîtresse
Dans les amitiés

I wish that the rose
Was still on its stem
I wish that I and my love
Were still together

Il y a longtemps que je t'aime
Jamais je ne t'oublierai.

I loved you a long time
Never never forget you.

The SINGER and his INTERLOCUTOR go; enter AGNES.

AGNES performs what minimal stage management jobs there are, and then tells us:

AGNES: Six months later. (Exit.)

ANNIE takes her place at the table as soon as it is ready.

MARION comes in from the other side (the 'outside').

MILTON (off): A-annie! Marion! Hallo, hallo!

ANNIE: Can you hear him? He's out of bed again: funny how you can tell, but you can.

MARION: Yes.

ANNIE: Go and see what he wants.

MILTON: A-annie!

ANNIE: Go on.

MARION: You go, he's your husband.

ANNIE: I don't know what that's supposed to mean; he's your father as well isn't he? Get out of here and see what he wants.

MARION goes off.

ANNIE (to us): Bloody bleating away up there: he's some money somewhere, and I know, and he knows I know. He's just trying to torment me. He managed to get out of bed not so long ago, and I found him in the entry: he must have had it hidden there. My saints he's a buggeroo. At least I can be thankful he's frightened of being parted from it, I know it's in the house somewhere. He's got me in such a state that I can't think at all: Where the hell can I look? I said I was looking for some tights I'd lost and rooted through every single drawer in the bedroom, and he just lay there looking at me without flickering an expression; I could have saved my energy, 'cause I knew for sure it wasn't there if he was just letting me look. Smirking there inside of himself. He knew.

MARION returns, taking out her car keys as she crosses.

ANNIE: And where d'you think you're off to?

The phone begins to ring. ANNIE takes it.

MARION: Eh? Well he wants me to go for Auntie Martha; fetch my sister he says, I'm dying, I've something she must know. He should be on telly my Dad.

ANNIE: Wait a minute Marion, don't you go. (On the phone.) Yes, I heard you, yes. Now. Yes Central Station. Be along in twenty minutes. Thank you. (Rings off.) I'll go for Martha, there's a car wanted Central Station, he's waiting now. Name of Evans. Said he'd wait in the..

MARION: He asked me to get Auntie Martha.

ANNIE: Yes, I heard you say so, I'll get her. Hurry up now: Mr Evans, said he'd wait in the buffet.

MARION: I know what'll happen, you won't go, and he'll take it out of me; he said I'd to go.

ANNIE: What does he care who goes? I said I'll go and I will; where's Agnes?

MARION: She's washing down the twenty seater.

ANNIE: Tell her to come in here to me, the bus'll take no harm to be left.

MARION goes.

ANNIE: Ooh. Ooh. It's as if he could hear through floorboards; sending for her now. He'll tell her where he's got his money hidden. It's only badness; unless he knows something or suspects. No, he's always had a nasty turn of mind, he's just tormenting me. He'll have his own family dealing with his money or else no one; well I'm not having it. And supposing it gets lost? Nobody'll know where the bloody hell it is. My saints he's a buggeroo.

MRS MATHER enters.

MRS MATHER: Morning Annie my love.

ANNIE: Mrs Mather, am I glad to see you.

MRS MATHER: You are in a state aren't you?

ANNIE: You wouldn't believe the mess I'm in with Milton.

MRS MATHER: Oh? And I heard he was doing ever so well.

ANNIE: He's going fast.

MRS MATHER: There now. You'll be worried then; all the arrangements business dealings and such. Mm.

ANNIE: He's always been a buggeroo but he's excelling himself.

MRS MATHER: It's always awkward for a woman; you want to make sure everything's in order.

ANNIE: That's just it Mrs Mather; his bloody money. He's never trusted anyone, least of all me; and certainly not the Income Tax. And now he's sent for his sister Martha.

MRS MATHER: Yes, I know who you mean. You'll be concerned about that; I mean they take against you at the last you know; those who've least call. Of course he could have handed it over to someone already.

ANNIE: No he hasn't; I've been watching his every move.

MRS MATHER: I expect he'll have it hidden somewhere; you want to look around a bit; I'm sure you're entitled. If you have to go wresting it back off his side of the family it'll have to be declared and then all sorts of complications could happen.

ANNIE: He keeps damn shifting it from one place to another; I see him at it, and he thinks I don't; but what can I do? I can't do nothing.

MRS MATHER: I've known women to regret it all their lives that they wasn't properly disposed. What a worry for you.

ANNIE: He keeps the finance company at bay with dribs and drabs and what he's forced to pay them on the cars; if he parks out that money and I can't get my hands on it they'll snap at a chance to sell every vehicle we've got from over my head; there'll be nothing.

MRS MATHER: You don't want that, not after what you've had to put up with; no woman would.

MILTON (off): Annie!

ANNIE: Don't Mrs Mather; what can I do? I'm on my own here, I really am. Nick's afraid to get involved. . .he said yesterday it was under the boards in Milton's room.

MRS MATHER: There now; anyone else'd have had a look.

ANNIE: How could I do that, with him lying there in the room?

MRS MATHER: Mmm.

ANNIE: No chance; I'll see it on him one day, then next time I look he's got without it and I don't know where.

MRS MATHER: You want to be careful you don't regret this all your life. (Glances innocently about for eavesdroppers:) How about pills? Is there anything he takes? You know.

MILTON (from offstage): Annie!

A DRIVER enters to collect his key from the table drawer.

DRIVER: Morning Mrs Peters; that Mr Peters shouting? How is he?

ANNIE: It's just him coughing, that's how he sounds. He's very low.

DRIVER: What the doctor say?

ANNIE: Milton won't tell him anything or be of any help; he says he's dying, clams up when the doctor comes, and the doctor's no sooner gone than he's out of bed.

DRIVER: I saw him at the window: he looked bad.

ANNIE: He's frightened the doctor won't let him have the pills he likes.

MRS MATHER: He should let the doctor do his business.

ANNIE: They're only some sort of pep pill. The doctor presribed him some.

MRS MATHER: Yers, course they are, he wouldn't refuse that.

DRIVER: You've had a toil with him Mrs Peters.

ANNIE: It's endless.

MRS MATHER: It's all very well if you're young, but what happens when you're left old.

DRIVER: Eh?

MRS MATHER: Old age is a prison, and that's a fact. You want to see things is left right Annie.

DRIVER: Oh.

MRS MATHER: Be sure the doctor comes tomorrow love, the way he is. Did you hear Marie Lees married Mathew Thornton?

DRIVER: Sorry? Were you speaking to me?

ANNIE: That's nice.

DRIVER: Mathew Thornton? Works at Rome Mill? I know him. He's a widower isn't he?

MRS MATHER (nods): Got four of his own. Married Marie Lees he has.

DRIVER: That's handy for him then. Yer, I know who you mean.

MRS MATHER: We went round for us tea; you couldn't refuse.

DRIVER: Pardon?

MRS MATHER: They'd neither of them had much to offer, so I daresay they'll suit each other very well.

DRIVER: I'll get down to the car then. .

ANNIE: Right.

MRS MATHER: Are you going then?

DRIVER (comes back to look at this phenomenon): Yes. (Goes.)

ANNIE: Shurrup about them pills. He's bloody starving Mrs Mather, starving himself. One of the drivers put him onto a feller that got him hundreds, and he's got them hidden up there.

MRS MATHER: Fancy, they're cunning. .

ANNIE: I said shurrup, I wish you'd never put it into my head.

MRS MATHER: Now what's this? I don't know what you think you're leading up to Annie Peters, but don't you drag my name into it. You're beside yourself, and it's no wonder, and everybody knows it.

ANNIE: He can't leave 'em alone, God knows how many he takes.

MRS MATHER: Just ordinary pep pills darling, thousands take 'em.

ANNIE: I said bloody shurrup about them: be told.

MRS MATHER: It's all right Annie love, I know you're overwrought, and you've got the business of the money on your mind as well; what a world we live in.

ANNIE refuses to respond.

MRS MATHER: It'll be your last chance, this.

ANNIE: He's sent for his sister; I said I'd go. I'd better.

MRS MATHER: Have I to go up and see how he is?

ANNIE: I tell you I've looked everywhere; anyway he'll have his eye on you.

MRS MATHER: I don't know what you mean Annie Peters; but I'll tell you this; I've learnt to accept things as they are I have, and not as they might be; I recommend you to do the same. (Sets off towards the indoor exit, stops and returns.) I'll just see how he is, and if I find anything out, you'll be glad I daresay. Whatever you've got into you head about those pills, I shouldn't mention it to Nicky darling: he could go off you. He's very good hearted, couldn't kill at chicken. .

MILTON, a death's head, at the inner door; his eyes misty.

MILTON: Nobody listens when I shout.

ANNIE: What are you doing downstairs? Get back to bed!

MILTON: Has the girl gone for our Martha? I'm in a bad way; I want to see our Martha.

ANNIE: Marion's had to go on a job; I've sent for Agnes; I can't go and leave the office altogether empty; I'll go as soon as I've a chance.

MILTON: You never come near; I couldn't reach my pills; that's the only thing helps me; and no one gives me so much as a drink.

AGNES enters carrying a full shopping bag.

ANNIE: Agnes, your Dad's got an errand for you.

MILTON: Agnes?

AGNES: Yes Dad?

MILTON: Go to your Auntie Martha's, tell her I want to see her, I need to see her.

AGNES: Just that?

MILTON: Say she's to come here as quick as ever she can, that I've not long.

AGNES hands over the shopping to her mother, and goes.

AGNES: I'll be there as quick as I can. (Exit.)

MRS MATHER: Now then Milton, are you going to sit you down?

MILTON: Mrs Mather is it?

MRS MATHER: Give Mrs Peters a chance to straighten up your bed... away you go Annie darling. I'll answer the phone if it rings.

MILTON creeps into the room. ANNIE waits till he's passed her and hurries off.

MILTON: Annie? Where's she got to?

MRS MATHER: What's that Mr Peters? She'll be back in a minute. Why don't you sit down? Look at the state of you: just bones; wait till I tell my Mr Mather, he'll be shocked.

MILTON: It's only a matter of time.

MRS MATHER: Now there's no need for you to talk like that; you've had the doctor and he'll do all he can. You can thank your stars you've a good wife who'll see to things, if you'll give her the chance; I only hope you've made the proper arrangements with her that's all. Have you informed the Bank? For if you get any sicker?

MILTON: Bank? What Bank? They know nothing, I tell 'em nothing. Keep my money where I can see it; I expect she has told you.

MRS MATHER: Told me what? Annie's said nothing to me I can assure you.

MILTON: So what's all this about a Bank? Where is she? Annie!

ANNIE (off): Yes?

MILTON: Where's Annie got to!

ANNIE: Agnes's gone! I'm making your bed! Will you come to it?

MILTON (subsides, only barely aware that ANNIE's replied): I'll sit here awhile; don't suppose I'll have another chance.

MRS MATHER: What a way to talk. .

MILTON: You shut it Mrs Mather: malignant old bletherer; you might fool Annie, but you don't me. It's suffocating in that bedroom, oppressive. My heart does beat, pounds it does; I think I must miss some of what's going on, it's so loud. What?

ANNIE reappears.

ANNIE: Well? Are you coming to your bed or not? Milton! Milton!

MILTON just sits there, unmoving, listening to his own heart.

MRS MATHER: He's all right Annie love, just overcome for a moment the lamb. You had your chance then, to do his bed, you'd be glad of that.

ANNIE shakes her head.

ANNIE: Could be in the loft; I caught him on the top landing yesterday, God knows how he got there.

MRS MATHER (referring to MILTON): Says he's not long; I'm inclined to believe him; see his nails are blue, and look at the colour of him.

NICK comes in. They all look down at Milton, who opens his eyes. He raises his right hand weakly, the index finger curled against the thumb. Flicks the finger; gazes mistily about to see who's there.

MILTON: Tokyo, 1964: putting the shot. No casualties.

NICK: Hallo Mum, how's Dad?

MRS MATHER: We're managing, thank you darling.

NICK: He looks rough, doesn't he?

MILTON: That you Nicky? Come here while I speak to you.

NICK goes over.

MILTON: Have you nothing to do?

NICK: What? Oh there's no jobs on just now; I've done the schools' bus. You do know what time o' the day it is?

MILTON: Did you bleed the brakes on the eight wheeler? They need it.

NICK: It's half past nine in the morning Mr Peters, and anyway how the hell d'you know they want bleeding?

MILTON: They needed bleeding ten days ago when I took to my bed, and you never move without I tell you to. There's a window in that bedroom you know. (Creeps over to the ledger to consult it blearily and from an inch off.) You just walked away from it; it's not two minutes of a job, you could have done it before you came back in here. Now you'll still have it to do and it'll take up twice the amount of your time.

MRS MATHER: Nick, you can do better than that I know; just consider how Mr Peters is; it's up to you to take the weight and strain off while he's not himself.

MILTON: Monkey nuts. (Having consulted the ledger:) Nothing for an hour, just your chance to fix those brakes, away and do it Nick; Annie, see to the phone for a while. Nick, you could get a couple cars washed down while we've a chance, they'll rot under all that muck, get both the girls to help you. (Pauses, dizzy..) Ouf, I'm that weak.. Tarah Mrs Mather, if you're going.

MRS MATHER (humorous with it): Way you talk Mr Peters, I'd say you wanted us all somewhere you know, while you got on with some private business.

MILTON: I bloody do. Has Nick gone?

NICK: I'm just going.

MILTON: Hold on a second. I shan't likely see you again lad, look after yourself.

NICK: You what?

MILTON (broken, weeping): Look after yourself Nick, think well of me.

MRS MATHER helps the weeping old man into the house.

NICK: Goodbye Mr Peters. (Quietly to ANNIE:) My word that was very impressive: he knows. I feel quite moved.

ANNIE: He's sent for his sister, he's got something up his sleeve; what was your idea saying he'd got his cash under the floorboards? Has he?

NICK: What? He might have, I saw him messing about in there. Why? He was crying, did you see? He was serious.

D'you think he knows about you and me? I should be sincerely sorry to hurt his feelings you know.

ANNIE: What the hell's bothering you? He's treated you like muck and you know it: you owe him nothing; you realise he was all for sacking you? You want to turn your thoughts to me a bit.

NICK: You? What for? When he's dying?

ANNIE: He's dying, and he's aiming to stash his money where we can't get it.

NICK: Is he? I had a feeling he knew something: that's rotten. Fancy going to your death with that on your mind.

ANNIE: Oh Nick, Nicky darling, pay attention: he's sent for his sister, he'll put it in her hands: he's always trusted her. There's only him knows how much there is, but it's plenty, because he won't be doing with banks and he pays his every bill on the last warning. We've got to get it before he gives it to her: I can't last here two minutes without cash.

NICK: Annie, rob a dying man, I don't know what you're thinking of: it's not decent.

ANNIE (contained fury, quiet): I'll give you bloody rob; without that money I might just as well walk out of that door and forget everything; it's mine, and it's not robbery to get it.

MRS MATHER (as she enters): There now, he's settled. It's round his neck Annie, what we was mentioning; he's a curious old feller isn't he. Mm. Parcel, on a string, under his shirt. He's comical. Go and look.

ANNIE: I'll go when I'm ready. In a minute.

MRS MATHER: He says he'll take his pills, says they pull him round.

ANNIE: He doesn't know what's going on when he's taken enough of those; and God knows he takes enough.

MRS MATHER: There now; you go and see to him in a minute; Nick'll wait here.

NICK: What for?

MRS MATHER: You'll look after the phone a minute, and then you can take this packet Annie'll give you and make sure it's well hidden.

NICK (mutters, frightened): I don't want to.

MRS MATHER: Seems nobody wants to do anything in this house.

NICK makes for the door.

MRS MATHER: Nick! I shall want a word with you, stay where you are; Annie's just got a bit of business to attend to.

NICK: I'm going to fix those brakes, I want no part of this.

MRS MATHER: Nick, d'you hear me?

AGNES comes in.

ANNIE: Well?

AGNES: She was at her daughters, she's coming directly she says.

ANNIE: That's settled then.

Pause.

AGNES (regards the wooden faces): What's up with everybody?

ANNIE: Agnes, your father says will you wash down those two cars outside.

AGNES goes back out.

AGNES: There's some queer people honest.

ANNIE summons up the remainder of her courage and walks slowly to the house door. Exit.

MRS MATHER: She's just got a bit of business to attend to. I'm glad of a moment of conversation with you Nicholas, so just pay attention a minute would you darling?

NICK: I know what she's gone doing; and she's no right to.

MRS MATHER: Yes darling I know; but we can't interfere with that though can we? I mean that's between husband and wife.

NICK: I expect so; yes, I get your point; you've got to be sensible about these things, and discreet.

MRS MATHER: Will you do just one thing for your mother

Nicholas?

NICK: I will if it's physically possible.

MRS MATHER: You be the one that sees her through this trouble; don't let anybody else.

NICK: Oh yes, certainly I'll do what I can. She's been extremely good to me.

MRS MATHER: You know what's going on; and I know what's going on; if she's to keep her head above water she's going to need all the help she can get from a strong trustworthy man.

NICK: What d'you suggest?

MRS MATHER: Just show yourself helpful; be there, an arm to lean on. Make sure she knows who her friends are, that's all we can do. If you're here, steady and true, she won't turn against you as she might, considering.

NICK (stares at her for a moment): Considering what?

MRS MATHER: You don't imagine she's going to be able to manage here all on her own, with nobody to take decisions and dispose the money and such, do you?

NICK: Oh come off it Mum, bloody hell he's not dead yet.

MRS MATHER: These things have to be faced, we're none of us immortal you know. There's the girls to be thought of as well and their share. If she marries again they have to be considered, being his daughters.

NICK: You're too devious for me; I don't know what you're getting at at all.

MRS MATHER: Don't you try to insult me young man, we must consult what's right and best that's all. Don't think it's been any pleasure to me what you've been up to with Annie Peters, another man's wife. Well, your chance'll soon be here to put that right, I just don't want you missing it. Married women's property applies to fellers as well, I had a consultation with a solicitor.
I could easily have said this many a long month ago, but I kept quiet. When she comes down those stairs, you attend to her my lad; she'll need it, the shock.

NICK (self-conscious laugh): All right then I will, that's only human isn't it? Satisfied?

MRS MATHER: That's right Nicholas, we're all human: that's a very good way of putting it. Thank you.

NICK: That's not what I bloody said and you know it.

MRS MATHER: No but it's what you meant I'm sure.

NICK claps his hand to his head in frustration.

ANNIE enters. She has a tight bundle of notes in her hands, wrapped in well-worn brown paper and tied up with string. She is shocked, and can't speak for a moment.

MRS MATHER: Oh. There now, you managed it. You'll want someone to look after that for you for the moment.

ANNIE doesn't move. Nor does NICK.

MRS MATHER: Is Milton all right? He didn't look well at all. Nicky, see to Annie.

ANNIE: Ladies and gentlemen, I have some extremely sad news to tell.

MRS MATHER: Oh now, Annie, oh dear. Nicky, make her sit down, she's shocked.

NICK moves to ANNIE, but her stillness and indifference puts him off making her sit.

The parcel dangles in ANNIE's hand, and eventually NICK takes it to save it falling to the ground.

MRS MATHER: Now just take care of that Nicky, she's not herself; that is a lot, my word it is, choke a cash register that would.

ANNIE: He, my husband, Milton Peters, of Peters' Taxis, has just recently died, at the age of fifty. I thought you'd want to know.

MRS MATHER: Only fifty, what a shame. I thought he was older; of course he had been very poorly.

ANNIE: He was ill for some time, as you know, but seemed a little better of late. He was up and talking at nine-thirty a.m., but complained of fatigue and retired after a short while.

MRS MATHER (discreetly and quiet, re the wad): See it's somewhere safe now Nicholas. Nicky'll look after it darling, don't give it another thought; I think you'd better go and lie down; I'll speak to Martha when she comes.

ANNIE: When I went to his room a few minutes later he was quite still, and there was no pulse. The only other surviving relative, his sister, Martha, arrived just after the end and called a doctor at once, who confirmed the death and issued a certificate. We were married for twenty-one years. He leaves a widow and two unmarried daughters.

NICK takes her arm, and she allows herself to be led into the house.

MRS MATHER (to us): My Nicholas will see she has everything she wants before he gets back to his work.
There will now be an interval of. . . . minutes. (And she goes, the street way.)

## Act Two

AGNES prepares the stage, mopping where it's got marked or dusty.

The mirror-ball begins to turn, and the SINGER enters:

SINGER (sings): Late nights and shaky white days
Ain't drinking takes away my bright eyes
Ain't bad living gives me my grey face

This jockey drives late nights yes sir
This jockey drives late nights
I see a shadow of a running man
On my windshield there's a shadow there
There's a shadow of a running man.

Hire-car jockey goes rocking by
So tired maybe the eight-wheel coach tonight
Cigarettes and diesel rank tea and petrol

This jockey etc...

Oh that tinkling key that jails me
Takes away my days stoned-out
Cat's eyes snake on... sparks-from-the-big-knife-grinder

This jockey etc...

'man at the wheel says nothing
Locked up in thunder this man
Clock don't go from way back, gave up

This jockey etc...

Two matchsticks hold my lids up
Boys like the mouse in the wheel he says
One day I'll reach the end of this long journey

This jockey drives late nights yes sir
This jockey drives late nights
I see a shadow of a running man
On the windshield there's a shadow there
There's a shadow of a running man.

The SINGER goes.

AGNES (indicates the room to us): Same old place; almost a year later though. My mum married Nick Mather of course. She's daft: everlasting moaning, so I don't know what she did want.

The radio link burps a few times.

ANNIE enters and answers the burps.

ANNIE (into the radio): No, nothing until that call at seven-thirty, 23 Albery Road, for the Throstle.

The radio burps out an acknowledgement and goes quiet.

MICHAEL enters, in his forties, dark suit and chauffeur's cap, a one time drunk.

MICHAEL (to us): They call me Michael; and they could be right. Ouf! that's a lazy wind out there: it goes through instead of going round yez. Is the man feller not back yet?

ANNIE: Who's that you mean?

MICHAEL: Nicky.

ANNIE: No.

MICHAEL: Boozing again; he's an extraordinary feller.

ANNIE: Did somebody do the schools?

MICHAEL: What d'you think? I couldn't leave them poor bairns standing in the cold, and I knew he wasn't about the place. Took St Xavier's early and just managed the Chorley Street kids before they froze to the pavement. But still and all he should be back by this.

ANNIE: Money in his pocket, he'll be taking Marion round the clubs I daresay.

MICHAEL: That's the time for drinking, when you've money in your pocket, the only and the best time; money in your pocket and there's not much you can't get in town, oh my God yes.

AGNES: I heard 'em go Mum; he says he's going to buy her some fancy tights he says, I heard him; you say which you want he says. She has on her best coat and boots, you should ha' seen her. I wouldn't dress like that: wouldn't want to.

ANNIE: She goes out like a tart. Once she's outside this house she's more like a tart than a decent girl. Sitting in clubs.

MICHAEL (lowers himself wearily into a chair): Oh you're a hard woman Mrs Mather, you very seldom give anyone the benefit. Why not look on the bright side?

ANNIE's face.

MICHAEL: A man has a hard time of it making a living for himself: do not begrudge him when he relaxes a bit afterwards.

ANNIE: He's been relaxing since ten this morning: there was no hard time beforehand that I noticed.

MICHAEL: There you are you see, he doesn't even have a hard time beforehand; I wouldn't begrudge him that, not me. Good luck to him I'd say. (Slumps into a doze.)

ANNIE: Oh shurrup you, you're bloody mental.

The DRIVER comes into the room.

DRIVER: Is he not back yet?

ANNIE: No.

DRIVER: I wanted to see him about something; what time did he say he'd be back? D'you think perhaps he's in the Club? There's any number of cars outside, I didn't notice his though. People from town mostly at this time.

ANNIE: Agnes. Agnes d'you hear me?

AGNES: What is it Mum?

ANNIE: One of these days you'll fall off that broom and break your neck.

AGNES: I was just leaning on it.

ANNIE: Go to the Club and ask if your father's there. If he's drunk that's where he'll have ended up maybe.

AGNES goes and gets a coat to go outside.

DRIVER: I saw him and Marion going off together this morning, and I haven't just managed to catch him since.

ANNIE: You wouldn't would you? That's his reason.

DRIVER: You what?

ANNIE: It's on her account he keeps digging up some excuse to go into town. This that and the other, but the only reason is her and her nonsense.

DRIVER: Oh? Who?

ANNIE: Marion.

DRIVER: Did I say something?

ANNIE: Not so far as I know; it's not you it's him.

AGNES (on her way out): What have I to say if he's there?

ANNIE: Just see if he's there that's all.

MICHAEL (jerks awake suddenly): Jesus Mary and Joseph! (Stares wildly about him.)

DRIVER: Bloody Norah.

MICHAEL slides into sleep again.

DRIVER: Crikey he gave me a jump. I'd forgotten there was anybody else.

ANNIE: There was a lad, from Meekham.

DRIVER: Oh yes? From Meekham eh?

ANNIE: But he got the wind of what was going on here; they went out a couple of times, and then he gave up. What was there for him? Then there was the Whitehead lad.

DRIVER: Where?

ANNIE: Where what?

DRIVER: Where was the Whitehead lad?

ANNIE: Here. After our Marion, same as that lad from Meekham.

DRIVER: Persistent was he?

ANNIE: Who?

DRIVER: The lad from Meekham.

ANNIE: I don't think you're listening. Geoff Whitehead's Mum and Dad came round here the one time; but they've only to ask round here, you know that; they soon put the block on, for final.

DRIVER (hopes he's saying the right thing): Oh well, that's how it goes.

ANNIE: If you knew how they'd strung me along.

DRIVER: Who's that now?

ANNIE: Nicky and Marion; I was that fond I saw nothing, I

never suspected a thing; I went and bloody married him, and all the time they'd already made their arrangements previous.

DRIVER (after a moment): The Whiteheads?

ANNIE: What Whiteheads?

DRIVER: I don't know.

ANNIE looks at the DRIVER for a moment, a stranger. She passes a trembling hand over her brow.

ANNIE: And he's knocking me about; one time he might play the gorilla a bit when he'd had a few, but he never laid a finger on me, always goodnatured with it. But now, when things go wrong, drunk or sober it's me that gets it; got both hands in my hair the other day and... (Can't speak for a moment.)... and Marion's got a tongue like an adder.

DRIVER: I see, yes, well I'll be off now, to the car. Call back.

ANNIE: The first was an obstroculous old bugger, but I could at least get my own way with him once in a while; but not with this one. What chance has a woman got? You can't be young and desirable all your life; nobody expects a man to do that; it's as if you had to depend on someone's bloody _kindness_, bloody _charity_, to have anybody even _like_ you; you should be saying hard luck old chap or some such, and you're just embarrassed aren't you?

DRIVER: Oh I wouldn't say that... actually I'm very much in favour of women myself.

ANNIE: I've only to look at him, and all my spite just evaporates, he takes the guts out of me, I love him so much d'you see, he gets me down here.

The DRIVER would rather be anywhere than here, but is riveted by the spectacle and indecency of her grief.

ANNIE: And there's the money; my word I slipped up there, my word I most certainly slipped up there.

MR MATHER appears in the doorway.

MATHER: Hallo? Evening everyone. How's Annie?

DRIVER: You asking me? Because I don't know.

MATHER: Mm? I wasn't asking anyone. Don't know what?

DRIVER: You said 'How's Annie?'

MATHER: I expect I did.

The DRIVER crumples his hat in one hand and passes it to the other and back again.

DRIVER: I came to speak to the boss; I had some conversation with Mrs Mather here; then you came in and said 'How's Annie?' I understood the question, but I couldn't answer it. I'm going back to the car.

He goes, a worried man.

They watch him go.

MATHER: It's about the van. I wanted a word with Nick, is he in just now?

ANNIE: He's in town.

MATHER: On a job? How long will he be?

ANNIE: I couldn't say.

MICHAEL starts awake again and stares wildly about him.

MICHAEL: Jesus Mary and Joseph!

MATHER: What? Oh. Michael: what a surprise.

MICHAEL: Ah, oh, er, how are you these days.. Albert old chap.

MATHER: I've come to see Nicky, he's in town.

MICHAEL: I know.

MATHER: Yes. Mm. How are you these days?

MICHAEL: I'm off the bottle completely these days Albert: given it up don't you know. But it's not much of a place that I have, and Annie here knows it, so she lets me hang around here especially if it's cold. Which it is.

MATHER: No but I mean, what you doing here in the first place.

MICHAEL: Driving for your Nicky.

ANNIE: Nicky has better things to do with his time these days than drive a motor, so he's hired Michael as well.

MATHER: I thought you said he was on a job just?

ANNIE: I said he was in town. I didn't say he was on a job.

He's boozing, for a pound.

MICHAEL: Now what's wrong with that I ask you, if he has the money in his pocket.

MATHER: Oh now, that's not right; first kill the pig I mean.

ANNIE: He's a pig all right.

MICHAEL: Now you're very harsh on him Mrs Mather darling.

ANNIE: It's him that's harsh on me.. sorry Mr Mather I didn't mean to say that in front of you.

MATHER: Oh, it's like that between you, is it. I see. You do things for the best; I was quite glad for you and him to marry, for him to help you out here. I thought he'll settle now; and look how it turns out. Money never did anybody any good.

MICHAEL: Fat'll drive a dog mad; see me, when I had money in my pocket: drunk for three weeks I was. Remember Albert? I was the lad wasn't I? Last time I pawned my suit, and when that was all drunk I went teetotal. I had to borrow a jacket and trousers to get to the Labour Exchange. Where's your shirt? says the clerk. Glory be, in my eagerness to get out of the way of the feller whose clothes I'd borrowed I'd forgot to don my own shirt. Oh them was the days.

MATHER (not following MICHAEL too well): How's the wife Michael?

MICHAEL: Oh her, she's found her own level. As you get older you don't bother your head so much about that sort of thing do you? You'll see her round the more salubrious bars looking very smart: one side of her face has a sort of droop on it, and like as not she'll have one eye darker than the other or else maybe closed up for style. Never sober, the darling.

MATHER: Oh. That sounds bad. Is she all right?

MICHAEL: She likes being on her own; which is all well, for she hasn't the choice. She's found her own level; a woman on her own doesn't have much chance you know; not even a you-know-what, no matter what they say.

Pause.

MICHAEL: They get things wrong with their things don't you

know; and then where are they? No tool kit for the job.

Pause.

MATHER: What's he up to in town? On a job is he?

ANNIE: No, he's not on a job Mr Mather, I said not. He said something about going for cash at the bank.

MATHER: Cash? What cash? You've got cash coming in from jobs haven't you? What's he want cash for?

ANNIE: Oh it's only the schools' cheque; we don't touch the rest. About thirty pounds, that's all there is to come.

MATHER: All? Maybe that's all today, maybe. That's as maybe Annie my love. Yes. You want to be very careful over that 'all', tomorrow or the day after it mightn't be 'all', it could be the lot.

MICHAEL: All is the lot isn't it Albert? Not that it's any concern of mine.

MATHER: My meaning is the working capital, which you cannot do without.

MICHAEL: That's true enough; capital's the thing.

ANNIE: The money's safe.

MATHER: Ah that's just it; excuse me Annie, but he is my son. How can it be safe when he's drawing it? Just answer me that. That money's going to be needed, mark my words; new vehicles, repairs, licences, insurances. . M. O. T. , have you considered that?

MICHAEL: Albert, Annie's here; it's not her that's away spending money. It's embarrassing in front of me d'you know?

MATHER: Some part of every cheque is for earning that cheque again, you can't just draw it out, it'll sneak up behind you, and catch you out. If I take the day's money out of the till, who's to find me the price of tomorrow's stock? No: I wait until she's ready, and we count it together, and then we think about it.

MICHAEL: Oh you do right there Albert: if I'd done the same with my good lady, we'd be happy now. D'you know when I've worked for business people. . .

MATHER: Take thought for the morrow, Annie, that's all I ask. For your own sake as well as Nicky's.

ANNIE: I've no part of it; the bank manager advised Nicky the money'd be best in a deposit account and that's where it is. You get interest that way and your money doesn't go down. So that's what Nicky did.

MICHAEL: That's the greatest thing: to be a capitalist. D'you know when I've worked for business people, their work was half their money, the rest was just their money working for them? It's a wonderful thing that: everybody should be on that thing.

MATHER (struck): I wonder where does the money come from in the first place though?

ANNIE: It comes from the bank.

MATHER: Yes, but how does it get there?

ANNIE: Eh? People put it in, I just told you.

MICHAEL: People put it in, people pull it out; oh they'll get found out those banks, one of these days; telling everybody it's more.

ANNIE: It is more.

MICHAEL: All right if you say so Annie, I wouldn't want to put bad thoughts into your head; but like Albert says, it'd be curious to know where this more's coming from, unless they're manufacturing it. And I think that's criminal too. Though I could be wrong. Imagine arresting a bank, Jesus Mary and Joseph. I'll tell you how it goes will I?..

ANNIE: Oh you, you're bloody mental.

MICHAEL: Wait till I tell you, though you won't believe it. Now just you imagine, for the sake of argument, that you are the proprietor of a taxi service Albert, and I'm a rich capitalist. It's the slack time of the year, and just the time you could do with having the vehicles overhauled. D'you understand me? No work gives you the leisure to have the vehicles attended to, but no work equals you can't pay to have the vehicles attended to.

MATHER: It's extremely costly, dealing with motors...

MICHAEL: Dear Michael, says you to me, be so good as to advance me a few pounds, and when the summer coach trip money starts coming in you'll have it back. Meanwhile, when you need a ride, ask me. . that being what I deal in d'you see? Michael has money, Albert has motor rides, so they do a swap.

MATHER: You're not going to suggest that that's how banking works are you, bank loans and that?

MICHAEL: That's right Albert, it doesn't does it. No no I say, in my beautiful mahogany office, don't you put yourself to all that bother giving free rides to me, I might not want one for weeks. . . come to think of it I'm so incredibly rich I have a car of my own; no no, you just give me a few extra pounds when you repay the loan, and we'll call it quits.

MATHER: It's only sensible isn't it? There's no embarrassment: I hate owing anybody a favour don't you, I avoid 'em.

MICHAEL: Now, now Albert, see what happens next, if not beforehand. Annie here sees me walking along the street, or maybe riding in my magnificent motor, and she sees the cut of me suit and she says by Jesus that feller knows the handle and feel of money. Here's me, says she, with more than I can use at this instant, and yet I don't have half the cut of that beautiful feller Michael there. Would you see if you could look after my few pence Mr Michael sir she says, dimpling prettily. Certainly, I say, my pleasure, I know a certain taxi hire operator whose palms are wet with apprehension at this instant. Back I hurry to your garage, I apprise the business, and if there's a strong chance of you earning me and Annie that money and the modest percentage I had in mind, don't I come to you again, bountiful friend that I am, and bank loan and mortgage and life assurance you to your heart's content?

And where are you, Mr Mather?

MATHER: I'm not anywhere, I shall just have too much money for what I need.

MICHAEL: You won't have any money, Albert, you will have goods and debts; you will be over a barrel, spread bloody eagled. You'll be working away there, earning me my money back, the Lord bless and keep you.

MATHER: Well that's it isn't it? That's trade, it stimulates trade.

MICHAEL: You're right there. And the fascinating thing is, no matter how much you take away in armoured vans, no matter how much I lend to you, the banks are never empty. Are they Annie. I'm amazed at that.

ANNIE's saying nothing.

MICHAEL: Round and round goes the money, and everybody's got some.

MATHER: I haven't got money.

MICHAEL: Except you. I was going to mention that.

MATHER: Cheeky bugger. We're on this earth to do an honest day's work, you can say what you like. Educated people take advantage, but that's nothing to do with it, you have to do what's right. You think you're so bloody smart, and I daresay you are, but what I want to know is, if you're so smart, why aren't you rich eh? Answer me that. You think you're educated, oh yes, you were blind drunk for three weeks last thing I heard. Clever Dick.

ANNIE: Now then Mr Mather, Michael didn't mean to upset you.

MATHER: Perhaps he didn't, but he did. You're all the same these days; in my frank opinion the world's gone mad. Where I work now, the lavatories, new ones they've given me. There's hardly any work for a man in them, you could eat your dinner off the floor, and what's it all for? There's no pride in anything any more.

AGNES hurries into the room, her coat clutched to her.

AGNES: They're coming now.

NICK swings violently into the room and steadies himself.

MARION dumps a few parcels just into the room and departs again.

NICK: Annie!

ANNIE (to the others): Take no notice.

NICK: Who is it? Who's just arrived? Announce who's just arrived Annie Mather.

ANNIE: Now none of your messing, come in and shut the door.

NICK: Who's just arrived? Who is it? Tell the people!

ANNIE (goes to take his arm): All right, have it your own way: my man's just arrived. Satisfied?

NICK: That's it! Man! Hus-band! And what's this man's name?

ANNIE: Nicky love, it's very cold, shut the door at least.

NICK: My full name if you please!

ANNIE: Nicky Mather, now come into the room.

NICK: Very good, excellent; but not quite good enough, is it mm? The full name; if you please, come on.

ANNIE (to the others): Oh he's a devil, if I say Nicholas it's 'Call him by the name he's known by', and if I say Nicky I get this.

NICK: Say the man's name.

ANNIE (laughs ruefully): Nicholas Mather; give over now, please.

NICK: Tha's better; infinitely better. But is it good enough?

ANNIE drags at him to get him into the room.

NICK: No, no; now you've got to say which foot goes first when Nicholas Mather steps into the room. My word I'm weary I think I'll sit down no I won't.

ANNIE: That's enough now; you're letting the cold in d'you hear me?

NICK: Say which first comes foot goes first my darling: you've got to say that, come on, f'me.

ANNIE (to the others): There's no dealing with him really. (To NICK:) All right then, left first. Now come on love...

NICK: That's right! the left! Right! Who said that?

ANNIE: Come <u>on</u> Nicky, we're all freezing in here...

NICK: Which foot comes first! Speak!

ANNIE: We've done that Nicky.

NICK walks into the room. ANNIE shuts the door.

NICK: 'Course we have. Right. Who's this?

ANNIE: Yes, look who's here.

NICK: My lovely old Dad. Nothing wrong with that is there? Not ashamed of my own father am I? I can say how d'ye do to my own father I should think. (Sweeps an unsteady bow and holds out a wavering hand, uncertain of his welcome.) I hope you're in good condition?

MATHER: Look at the state of you; have you driven home like that?

The phone rings. ANNIE answers it.

NICK: I've had a few Dad, jus' few that's all. Met a friend and had a few. (Sudden.) Man has control of his environment! In control. (Mimes steering a car, stylishly.) When I've had a few drinks, I know what it's all about; hand to the steering wheel, brrooom. All this, all those motors, petrol, engines, road, etcetera, for me; otherwise why? The man at the wheel.

ANNIE (on the phone, makes notes): Yes, five minutes, yes. (Rings off. To NICK:) Why don't you go and lie down?

NICK: I've read all about environment, 'n a papers; I'm definitely against it. I'm in charge. Wife! say where I'm standing. Where is Nicholas Mather standing?

ANNIE: That's enough, it's very boring for everybody else you know. Go and lie down. (She shakes the slumped MICHAEL.) Michael..

MARION comes in burdened with two more carrier bags, she eases past NICK into the room and he shuts the door after her. She crosses and goes into the house without a glance or acknowledgement at the company.

MARION: Look at the state of these bags, you've thrown 'em every which way into the back of the car. I couldn't find that material at all.

ANNIE: Come on Michael, wake up..

NICK: The material? It's there, in the bag still. Michael! Annie's talking to you!

MICHAEL stirs and stretches reluctantly.

ANNIE: Michael? There's a job at Atkinson Street. Four people to the Ace of Clubs.

MATHER: Now no, Nicholas, he's weary, look at the man.

NICK (to MATHER): You what? (To MICHAEL:) Take the big car! Marion, have you left the keys in?

MARION (off by now): Well I haven't taken them bloody out for sure!

MATHER (to NICK): You've no business sending him out, there's a law; what's wrong with Marion going?

MICHAEL (mooches wearily to the door): Hallo Nicky, you're stoned again are you? I bet the car's in a mess. (To ANNIE:) What number Atkinson Street?

ANNIE consults her ledger note.

ANNIE: Fourteen.

MICHAEL goes with a wave.

NICK folds himself into the seat MICHAEL vacated.

NICK: Sorry Dad, sorry, I've had a few, sorry about that. But what d'you expect? You keep going and you keep going, bound to get on your nerves. The hand on the wheel, that's me. I'm in charge. Big responsibility you know, bound to get on your nerves. (Bawls.) Marion!

MARION (off): What?

NICK: Have you brought all the stuff in?

MARION (off): What stuff? I've brought mine in, whatever else there is is still in the boot! (Flings a parcel into the room.) Here, this isn't mine.

ANNIE (to NICK): Haven't you bought her enough stuff?

NICK: Don't be vexed Dad, it's just that I'm a bit overwhelmed at the moment, I can talk to you now, 'tend to any business you care to mention. You phoned about the money, tha's right. The van's shot...I 'member, don't think I don't. It can be arranged, all in hand. If you were talking about a huge 'mount, that'd be different, have to wait a bit. But as things are I can manage ever'thing you need. Right?

MATHER: Eh lad, ale's in..

NICK: And what's that supposed to signify? Wit's out? I'm perfectly capable Dad, don't think I'm not. Arrange ever'thing, you see; just give me chance. Have you never been a bit fuddled yourself? 'Course you have.

MATHER wags his head wearily.

NICK: I will, what's the matter with you? D'you think I won't or something? (Hoists out his wallet and counts out a wad of a hundred pounds. ) I don't understand your attitude at all, but whatever you say I'm not going to neglect my own father am I? Got to be rational about these things. (Gathers the notes and thrusts them towards his father. ) Go on, that's what you came for isn't it? Think it's dirty money or something?

MATHER (avoids the money): Nay Nick, there's no way of talking to you in this state.

NICK: I'd be fascinated to know what's wrong with you: bloody take it will you!

ANNIE (mutters, avoiding NICK's eyes): Can't you just behave yourself for an instant, and with your own father? Look at the way you carry on, in front of everybody. Some people are just bloody animals.

NICK swings aggressively towards her, but lowers his voice to the same low mutter.

NICK: And you can shut up and keep out of it; you're not a particle of use to me, I hope you're aware of that?

ANNIE: Ah well, we all have our moments don't we? Seems mine's gone.

NICK: Yes yes, those were the days weren't they? What happened I should be interested to know; seems the only way to get your marital rights with some women is not to marry 'em.

ANNIE: Don't 'some women' me, you; a prostitute'd be better for what you want out of a woman.

NICK: A man wants someone who'll perform for sure.

ANNIE: You're just gross.

NICK: All right, I'm gross. I am gross, so forget it; I'll sort myself out, don't you fret; don't imagine it's any pleasure to me that I get sexually aroused if you don't push my hand away.

ANNIE: Isn't that just you: don't you think I get bored with your everlasting groping?

NICK: How dare you speak to me like that? How dare you? I shan't hold any further conversation with you.

He turns back to the others for all the world as if this vituperative muttering hadn't taken place in the same room.

NICK: Dad, will you please take this money off my hands?

ANNIE: Take it Mr Mather, he won't rest till you do.

NICK: You're definitely trying to humiliate me; well I won't accept it, not from you not from anybody. I'm extremely proud and sensitive.

MATHER accepts the money, eyes averted.

MATHER: I never taught you to drink like that Nick.

NICK: That's more like it; if you pay it back, well and good; if not, not. I shan't complain, that's how I am, me. Where's Marion got to? (Bellows.) Marion! come here and show what I bought you!

MARION (off): What?

NICK: Show 'em what I got you!

MARION: What you got me? Who wants to see? Anyway I've put them away!

NICK: Fetch 'em out, d'you hear me? Show Agnes, she'll be interested; she likes nice things!

MARION reappears in the doorway, parcels in her hands.

NICK: Ah, there you are. Come on, unwrap 'em, give 'em here.

MARION slaps the parcels on the table.

MARION: There you are then, though I don't see what point.

AGNES unwraps one parcel, the tights, with reverence.

AGNES: Oh aren't they lovely. Mrs Chorley has some just like, only not so nice as these. Mum, can I have some soon?

MARION: Mrs Chorley? Who's she when she's at home - I bet she's got nothing like this then.. (Eagerly she undoes another parcel, a cashmere jersey.) Look at this, feel how soft: it's Italian.

AGNES: Oh, isn't it beautifully made? So light. It is pretty this.

NICK: Pretty, that's just what it is. Have to get you one o' those Agnes eh?

ANNIE: Have you finished littering up the table? (Rams the parcels together impatiently.)

NICK: Here, what's all this? Look what you're doing!

ANNIE: I'll give you look; d'you think we've never seen a pair of tights before? Get 'em out of the way! (Shoves them over on to the floor.)

AGNES: Ah no Mum, don't spoil 'em.

NICK (holds up the parcel that MARION threw at him): Annie! hey look!

MARION (rescuing her parcels and paper): Whose things do you think you're chucking about on the floor? You chuck your own things about.

NICK: Annie love! look what I've got here? (Holds up the parcel.)

ANNIE: Oh belt up Nicky, I've had enough for one night.

NICK: Did you think I'd forgotten you? Had I heck; just didn't get round to it, had it in my hand though, all the time see.

ANNIE pays reluctant attention.

NICK puts the parcel on his chair and sits on it.

NICK: Only you have to earn it. Where is your husband Nicholas Mather sitting?

ANNIE: Nick, please forget it will you? I said I've had enough.

MARION: I don't know why you bother with her at all Nicky, she's a begrudging sod.

ANNIE: And you can keep out of it Marion Peters: no doubt you're well aware of whose money you were pissing away all afternoon?

MARION: It would have been yours no doubt, if you could have got your hands on it: but you didn't did you?

ANNIE bars MARION's way as she tries to get by to take her parcels back into the house.

MARION: Out of my way.

ANNIE: Don't you shove me young madam, or you'll get a lesson in shoving!

MARION: Go on then, try it, that's all, and see what happens.

NICK (gets between them): Now then you two, that's enough. Give over.

MARION: Who started it then? (To ANNIE:) You want to keep your head shut you do, considering your past: it's a bit murky isn't it? Don't think I don't know, and a few more besides me!

ANNIE: Know what? Come on then, let's be having it, what's to know?

MARION: I know, that's all.

ANNIE: I haven't been messing with my own stepfather, I know that.

MARION: You bloody mare, I'll give you messing: what about my father then? Your husband eh? Milton Peters didn't die natural and nobody'll tell me he did!

The phone starts to ring.

ANNIE flings herself on MARION, screaming.

ANNIE: You cow! you flaming cow!

NICK hauls ANNIE off.

NICK: Think what you're doing Annie.. just be sensible..

ANNIE: I'll pull her eyes out!

NICK: Out with you. (Shoves towards the street.)

ANNIE: What're you doing? I'll not be put out of my own house!

NICK: Out, d'you hear me? And don't you dare come back either, until you're calmer and sensible.

NICK forces her out into the street, she clinging to him and screaming.

ANNIE: No! no! no! I shan't go I shan't!!!! I'm not to be turfed out of my own house you can't do that! What d'you think you're doing you swine you swine you swine! D'you think you'll get away with this? You see my God you'll see. You're not above the law you!!

The phone stops ringing.

NICK: Come on with you.

ANNIE: I'll get a solicitor, I'll fetch the police!! Help!

NICK (prizes her fingers loose): Out, I'm telling you.

He gets her out and jams his foot against the door.

ANNIE (off): I'll drown myself! I'll do away with myself!

NICK: Some hopes!

AGNES (in miserable tears): Oh Mum, poor Mum.

NICK: Now then Agnes love, she'll be all right, she'll be back. You go and make us some tea eh love?

AGNES goes out to the back.

MARION picks up her belongings.

MARION: Did you hear the bitch? The way she carried on? Give us that parcel, I'll rip her headscarf to pieces.

NICK: I've shut her out, what more d'you want?

MARION: See what she's done to my jersey; cow; if she hadn't got out of here I'd have marked her.

NICK: Oh hush up, what're you fussing about?

MARION: Bloody drab; you should have had more sense and left her alone; you should have sent her to hell in the first place. The house is mine by rights anyway, and the money; my father wanted me to have it, I know, and her making out to be the big cheese. I'm over twenty-one.

NICK: Now shut up Marion, you don't know what you're talking about, so just keep quiet d'you hear me?

MARION: Not much I don't; I won't abide her in the house. She'll have to get out, I'm not having her in the house, chucking her bloody weight about as if she was somebody; she ought to be locked up, that's what; she's past it, and it's affecting her mind.

NICK: That's enough! what's it got to do with you? Just don't take any notice of her, I'm master here, and what I say goes. My own master, yours and hers. (Wags two crossed fingers at her.) That's her and me, and she's underneath. (Goes rooting in the table drawer for milk and sugar.)

MICHAEL comes in.

MICHAEL: What's the matter with Annie out there? I couldn't get a word out of her.

NICK: Her and Marion.

MATHER: Come and sit you down Michael.

MICHAEL: Those two'll never get on in this world.

NICK: Where's the bloody sugar? Are we having this tea or not?

AGNES comes in with a teapot and mugs.

AGNES: Could you see to it Marion?

NICK: Where you going then?

AGNES: My Mum's out the back. She's crying.

NICK: Tell her to come in; tell her to bring that bottle from the sideboard, and we shall want some glasses.

AGNES: All right. Thanks Dad. (She hurries out.)

NICK (fishes in his coat pocket): Present for me an' all. (Pulls out a jar of mussels.) Good for you, mussels. Head-scarf for the old lady.. think I got everything. (Fingers blearily at his wallet, counting up as best he can.) Dad! tea's brewed, and we're going to have a drink of whiskey an' all! Hundred pounds to my old Dad, and the... (Fumbles and mumbles his way through the day's purchases virtuously..)

AGNES and ANNIE come in, with glasses and whiskey.

ANNIE (the whiskey): Where d'you want this?

NICK: Table. (Back at his wallet.) Been to the law have you? S'all right, row's over and done with, no malice. No more tantrums; sit down and let's have a drink. (Rises, leaving his seat, nodding her towards the parcel there.) There you are: present for you.

ANNIE takes the parcel and sits.

MATHER rises, thrusting out the money in his hand.

MATHER (to NICK): Here you are, take your money back. It's yours. I'm going.

NICK: Going?

MATHER: Yes, I am. I've no intention of stopping in this house.

NICK: But Agnes has just brewed tea.

MATHER: I don't care whether she's brewed tea or not; things here aren't right, you're behaving extremely badly Nicky: I'm off.

NICK: Ah now Dad, come off it; sit you down and have a cup of tea.

ANNIE: Don't go Dad, don't be upset; everything's all right now. I'm sorry you had to be here to see all that, but it's over now. Don't you be upset as well.

MATHER: I'm not upset, not upset at all; I hope I'm as broad-minded as the next man; but what I've seen and witnessed here tonight breaks my heart. It does that. Your foot's set on a course that'll bring you nothing but unhappiness.

NICK: Ah now Dad come off it: you're having such a whoopee time of it of course.

MATHER: At least I'm straight! with myself as well as with others.

NICK: Dad, Dad times have changed; everything's more modern nowadays; it's not just all work, you've got to have a bit of fun: work hard play hard.

MATHER: You neither work, play, nor have fun! you don't think what you're doing, any more than a rat in a sewer, you're content to squirm along in the slime, the way the slime goes you go; I never taught you that! What did I say that time, remember my very words that time!

NICK: You've said a lot.

MATHER: What I said over Marie Lees that time.

NICK: Oh Dad now come off it please, that's all in the past. Sit you down and have some tea.

MATHER: I said it catches up with you, that's what I said; and that's what's happening; I can't just sit here and say nothing: muck grows on muck; you did wrong thing then, and you go on and on. (Suddenly.) I will not sit down in this house!

NICK: Oh now look Dad, be sensible; where d'you think all this raving's going to get you? You've no right to come criticizing me in my own house; get off my back please, I'm a grown man, are you aware of that at all? Times have changed.

MATHER: You may be right at that; I've heard the young knows everything these days, I've read all about that, in the papers; and that's just what I do mean: you're ruining your life, and you want to listen to me before it's too late!

NICK: We're managing perfectly well without your chat thank you very much! and while we're on the subject, who comes to who for money?

MATHER: Money? Take it! I shan't keep it, my word no. I'd rather beg than take your money, here, take it back.

NICK: Will you have done! you're upsetting everyone. (He grips the hand in which his father is proffering the notes.)

MATHER (shrieks): Take your hand off me!! I will not stay! I'd rather sleep in a field than among this filth!! Goodbye to you! (Wrenches himself wildly free and goes, with the money.)

NICK: Phoo, what a bloody fuss; what was he on about?

MATHER reappears in the doorway, brandishing his fist, unaware that he holds the notes in it still.

MATHER: Come to your senses Nicky! think what you're doing! Wrecking your own life and others! (Exit.)

MICHAEL: Jesus Mary Joseph, he's an excitable old man isn't he?

NICK: I'm depressed now; can't we have the wireless for a bit of music?

The phone begins to ring.

MARION: Bloody Norah he's remembered his wireless; you took it to be mended you dope, this afternoon. I've poured you out this tea, d'you want it or not? (Goes, carrying her parcels away.)

NICK: No. I don't want anything. I do feel low. About as low as you can get.

The phone stops ringing.

NICK (going): I hate rows.

ANNIE and MICHAEL remain at their places, and AGNES resets the stage.

Meanwhile the SINGER enters to entertain us.

SINGER (sings): Oh take the leap oh take the plunge
Shun not the joys of marriage.

In one block of flats lived Syd's friend Alice
And our Syd lived with us

The flats is high the lifts was bust
So they courted at long distances.

Oh take the leap etc...

Syd stood upon the parapet
And Alice yonder there
The space was small between them yet
Th'abyss gave them a scare.

Oh take the leap etc...

He gaily leapt she gaily leapt
Each leapt to join each other
And e'en in mid-air twixt parapets
They knew they'd made an error.

Oh take the leap etc...

Syd's oaken arms reached out to catch
She threw her tender self
They passed like ships they missed their lips
And plunged into the depths.

Oh take the leap etc...

They met at last as the air rushed past
The descent was swift and horrid
Divided we stand, hand reaches to hand
But united we fall says Alice.

Oh take the leap oh take the plunge
Shun not the joys of marriage.

ANNIE leaves.

AGNES (to us): A few months later. Spring time. (She looks round for evidence of this.) (There is none.). Same old place though. Our Marion was supposed to get married to Geoffrey Whitehead today; only she's not so well.

MR WHITEHEAD comes in from the house. A heavy, elderly man, rosy with heat and food and drink. He's in his best suit and has a carnation in his buttonhole. A tumble of whiskey in his hand, which he sets down on the table.

MRS MATHER follows, also in her best coat and hat, and with a corsage of carnations.

AGNES (indicating MR WHITEHEAD to us): Mr Whitehead, father of the groom. (Goes.) 'lo Mr Whitehead, 'lo Mrs

Mather.

MRS MATHER: Isn't things going nicely Mr Whitehead.

WHITEHEAD: Well, we came here for a wedding, and we aren't having one, otherwise things are fine.

MRS MATHER: That's what I mean: considering. Lovely it's been. And everybody's so understanding.

WHITEHEAD (looks at her for a moment): I suppose I'll show most sense if I leave it to you womenfolk.

MRS MATHER: Well, yes, it's unfortunate but it'll all work out, you see; isn't she a bonny girl? None bonnier for many a mile is there?

WHITEHEAD: Certainly; I said to our Geoffrey, I said I'm glad at least you're marrying a lass with some beef to her.

MRS MATHER: Oops Mr Whitehead!

WHITEHEAD: Eh?

MRS MATHER: You don't half come out with some things you. I know what's on your mind, and it's no wonder, with the confusion; just trust our Nick, that's all.

WHITEHEAD: Now hold on Mrs Mather, my mind wasn't on money at all...

MRS MATHER: Well if it had been anybody'd've understood. Her father left her well fixed I understand.

WHITEHEAD: Your Nick mentioned a thousand pounds.

MRS MATHER: There now; it isn't every married couple starts with that is it? I'm sure you must be very pleased.

WHITEHEAD: It's very fair; you understand I'm only thinking about the lad; you have to do your best for your own.

MRS MATHER: Nick told me himself, though of course he doesn't generally discuss these things with me, but he told me that when old Mr Peters was at death's door, God rest him, it was his idea that Nick should come in and help Annie, and the money was to be Marion's.

WHITEHEAD: A thousand pounds?

MRS MATHER: Mmm. Course, a lot'd be tied up, in the business. But the cash; every penny Mr Whitehead. He's had to work hard Nick, my word yes, but he won't grudge your Geoffrey, not him.

WHITEHEAD: Nor Marion I should hope..

MRS MATHER:.. nor Marion neither not him.

WHITEHEAD: A thousand pounds for a taxi business..?

MRS MATHER: Quite right Mr Whitehead, I expect you're right in expressing your doubts like that. Old Mr Peters wouldn't leave Annie bereft now would he? Not his own wife.

WHITEHEAD: Quite.

MRS MATHER: I'm sure Geoffrey'll get his due, when it's due.

WHITEHEAD: ..Marion..

MRS MATHER: Marion yes, I meant Marion, of course. Such a bonny girl, don't you think so? I was a pretty girl myself once over; very vain over my hair I was, mm.

WHITEHEAD: What's to do with her?

MRS MATHER: Who's that then?

WHITEHEAD: Marion?

MRS MATHER: Oh it's something and nothing, I mean you saw, wasn't she a picture, in her gown and bridal veil an all? She has a really solid constitution that girl I shouldn't wonder, else how would she look as good? She'll be back on her feet tomorrow, or else in a day or two; these women's things are soon over don't you fret, and then the wedding can go forward as if nothing had happened.

The phone rings.

MICHAEL comes in and answers it and then NICK and some GUESTS and ANNIE file in, making their goodbyes.

GUEST (to MR WHITEHEAD): We think it's time we were off.

WHITEHEAD: Yes, right, I'm ready.

NICK: Goodbye now, hope you've managed to enjoy yourselves, in spite of the unfortunate hitch; there's two cars lined up ready.

GUEST: I only hope it's nothing serious Mr Mather.

NICK: I'm sure it isn't; Agnes is with her now; we'll get a doctor if she doesn't improve.

GUEST: Geoffrey said he'd come round tomorrow when I phoned.

NICK: I'll speak to him later; she'll be glad to see him as soon as she's over it; we'll soon have her right.

They all go towards the street.

AGNES comes through from the house to draw ANNIE aside.

AGNES: Mum...

ANNIE: What is it love?

AGNES: I don't want them to hear..

ANNIE (moves aside a little): Well? What is it you want? Why aren't you with Marion?

AGNES: She's gone into the bathroom. It's awful Mum, I don't know what's the matter with her; she's crouched down, and sweating and pale and she keeps saying 'I'll scream, I'll scream I will' and blood all over her chin from biting her lip. I'm sure you should get a doctor.

ANNIE: She'll have to wait, there's these people to see off; can't have a worse carry-on than we've had already.

MICHAEL finishes the phone call, jotting down the details.

AGNES: Oh Mum, I'm sure she's really bad, and she keeps getting angry and saying awful things; about us all having the reception with her in the next room; 'I shan't marry him' she keeps saying, ''cause I shan't be alive to do it, I'll bloody die on 'em' she says, swearing an all Mum. Oh Mum, she isn't going to die is she? I'm frightened, I wish you'd get the doctor.

ANNIE: I'm having no doctor in here for a hysterical girl. She's not going to die I tell you. Oh dammit I'll go and have a look at her. (She goes, followed by AGNES.)

NICK comes back in, having waved the GUESTS off.

MICHAEL: There's a job Dinefield, half an hour; I've written it down in the book.

NICK (weary): You get some rest, I'll do it if they're not back in time.

MICHAEL: That bloody room stinks to here with the liquor they've been partaking; gin, whiskey, rum, desperate fine stuff: it's a good job I'm on the temperance these days.

NICK (slumps into a chair): D'you hear what I say Michael?

MICHAEL: It's a good job there's me working hereabouts, and not allowing my thoughts to dwell on strong drink.

NICK gives up trying to get MICHAEL to rest, and lapses into gloom.

NICK: What a mess eh?

MICHAEL: Eh? Oh I know that; ach there's adoption socities isn't there? She's an awkward young madam though isn't she? I mean she must have known for heaven's sake, and she lets you go on booking the Registry Office and everything.

NICK: Keep your head shut won't you Michael?

MICHAEL: Jesus, it's no business of mine; you cover your tracks as best you can.

NICK: She let Geoffrey court her with as ill a grace as she thought he'd tolerate; she knows Annie wants to get shut of her; that's why she's playing up. But she can't stay here can she? it's a mess for sure. Go and have a lay down in there, get some rest.

MICHAEL moves out.

MICHAEL: That whiskey smells very strong in there d'you know?

NICK sits broody for a second.

NICK: What a mess. Extremely embarrassing.

ANNIE comes in.

ANNIE: What are you doing sat there?

NICK: Sitting.

ANNIE: Come on with you; we've got to move; she's had it.

NICK: Yes.

ANNIE: Come on then, we've got to get it out of here. My God she's a madam.

NICK: What can we do with it?

ANNIE: I'll tell you what we do, <u>and</u> you'll do it.

NICK: We can get it adopted can't we?

ANNIE: Oh yes, you set about that then: 'I'd like to arrange the adoption of my son by my stepdaughter, stick around Geoffrey, it'll only take three months. . ' Is that how you'd put it? You're the life and soul while the fun's going aren't you? Not so swinging when it comes to paying the bill it seems.

NICK: Well what can we do?

ANNIE: Get down in the cellar and dig a hole.

NICK stares at her. Tries to speak. Runs his two hands over his face.

NICK: No! No!

ANNIE: It's bloody dead you fool, it's all right; your mother's seen it and it's dead she says; she says dig a hole in the cellar floor.

NICK: Isn't there some other way of fixing it? Shouldn't the Police be informed of such a thing.

ANNIE: 'Some other way. . ' Seems there isn't any 'some other way'; you should have thought of some other way about nine months ago you should you dirty pig. Now do what I say.

AGNES comes in.

NICK: No!

AGNES: Mum, Mrs Mather's calling you; she doesn't want me; I think our Marion's got a baby, I swear I heard it cry. She's been fat for months, it's a baby Mum.

ANNIE: Oh shut up and mind your business; I daresay you heard those kittens from the garage. Get off with you to bed or I'll give you something to think about.

AGNES: No Mum, I'll swear to it. .

ANNIE flies at AGNES, spins her round and pushes her from the room.

ANNIE: I warned you, out! out! and not a peep out of you either. (She follows, chasing AGNES out. )

NICK: What a mess; women; oh my lord what a mess. Think about it nine months ago she says. . . fat chance. A standing prick has no conscience, huh. I did the right thing by her when her husband dies, did the right thing by her, naturally. Then she tells me about them pills, those bloody pills.. whose idea was that? It certainly wasn't mine.. like a nightmare, and it's continuing, a continuous nightmare... I went completely off her, curious that, completely lost interest in her sexually once I realized what had happened with her, for weeks. Then there's Marion. What a mess. Oh bloody hell women.

MRS MATHER comes in carrying a small trenching tool; she goes to the cellar door and opens it. Looks back at NICK.

The phone rings.

MRS MATHER: Annie says she's spoken to you Nicholas: she has hasn't she?

NICK picks up the phone.

NICK: What's that?

MRS MATHER: Answer the phone darling; I'll wait.

NICK (on the phone): Mather's Taxi Hire. Yes. Yes. Formby Avenue to Halton Towers. (Writing in the ledger.) Number four A. Thank you.. ten minutes. (Goes to the radio.) Yellow three?

The radio crackles and a garbled reply is given, NICK consults the ledger.

NICK (on the radio link): Can you do Dinefield, next twenty minutes? Over.

The radio crackles a garbled reply.

NICK (on the radio link); Hartfield Crescent, twenty-three, to the airport, over and out. Yellow two? Over. Yellow two? Over.

The radio gives out a reply of sorts.

NICK (on the radio link): Job at Formby Avenue, four A, over.

The radio crackles out a reply and falls silent. NICK stays staring at the radio.

MRS MATHER: I brought this spade through Nick; I expect you'll need it, for what you have to do.

NICK: Mum please...

MRS MATHER: Is this all right for the job eh? (The spade.)

NICK (turns to stare at the spade): That child's alive.

MRS MATHER: Now whatever put that into your head Nicholas?

NICK: I heard it cry Agnes heard it cry, she said so.

MRS MATHER: There now with all this worry; you'd hear anything I shouldn't wonder.

NICK: I didn't mean me, I meant Agnes. She heard it.

MRS MATHER: Did she? Well I expect she knows best what she heard herself; Annie did say there was some kittens though; how does she know it wasn't them eh? I mean she's not bright is she? Here Nicholas.. (The spade.) Take it off me.

NICK: It's dead then?

MRS MATHER: Well I'm sure I'm no doctor, nor would I ask to be, so I can't judge a thing like that. It's dead by all accounts, so that's it isn't it?

ANNIE comes in.

ANNIE: Well? Is there a hole ready?

MRS MATHER: Now you haven't gone and left poor young Marion alone have you? That's naughty, and what about the other matter?

ANNIE: It's there in the room; I've covered it over in case it makes a noise. Has he dug a hole then?

MRS MATHER: Just give him a moment; he's very considerably shaken and shocked. He'll need all his strength.

ANNIE: I won't have her in the house, not her nor her bastard; I'll go straight to the police and tell them everything soonest. I'm not going to go on living like this, and if I'm going down then you can all come with me.

MRS MATHER: Now then Annie think what you're saying.

NICK: There's nothing for you to tell.

MRS MATHER: Of course there isn't Nicholas, whoever said there was? She's worried to death with her problems, you can expect it.

ANNIE: I'll tell you what I'll tell them old Ma Mather shall I? How about where did his money go to? Who had that eh? I got him onto those pills didn't I?

MRS MATHER: Oh Annie love, don't go on like that, it's very painful...

ANNIE: You got me the first lot didn't you? Remember? You knew you knew you knew: You were accomplice to the fact!

MRS MATHER: Annie, please, what would anybody listening think?

ANNIE: Look at his Lordship now; you've gone your own way long enough, you've treated me like shit; well it's mine turn now; night after night I've worked here, and for what eh? For anything I've got in the bank? For my health and good looks? Get it done you bastard or by Christ I'll do as I promised; get hold of that spade and do it!

NICK: I'll do it if you'll only stop nagging for a second... (Turns towards the cellar door.)

ANNIE: Where's that bloody police whistle? (Drags open the table drawers.)

MRS MATHER: Oh listen to her Nicholas, she's completely beside herself, but I don't think she'll do anything really..

ANNIE (grabs the phone): I'll dial nine nine nine; murder and robbery, I'll tell them..

NICK: That's enough! I'm going aren't I?

MRS MATHER: Of course he will Annie, you know that, put the phone down now, you don't know what you're doing.

NICK goes, shutting the door.

ANNIE (still beside herself, although she sets the phone back on the rest): He's walked all over me; I know he's your son but by God he's given me hell Mrs Mather, and it's got to finish, it's got to finish, or I swear I'll go out of my mind, I swear it.

MRS MATHER: Of course, Annie love, anybody'd understand what you're going through, anybody. Just get back to poor little Marion, and in no time now you'll have everything back as it should be. Bring it here, if you want, straight away. It's not two minutes of a job to lift a flagstone.

ANNIE: Just so's he has a dose of what I've had remembering what I had with Milton, just once; I'll make him like it; I don't care what happens to me from now on Mrs Mather. (She goes.)

MRS MATHER (looks down the cellar steps): There now he's all but done; bring the afterbirth while you're about it I should. (To us now.) Annie's got a dreadful tongue, and a temper; my heavens the things we have to go through in this life. And at my age too; I've a right to some peace. She's been through hell no doubt. Hell on wheels. I just hope, once young Marion's out of the way of temptation, that he'll pay some attention at last to his mother and father; oh my heavens you love them and get little thanks; only hardship.

NICK reappears at the cellar door.

NICK: Come on with you, let's be having it; where is it? You're idling. Let's get the bloody job done.

ANNIE hurries in with a tiny bundle, wrapped and pinned in an old frock and a newspaper parcel.

MRS MATHER: Have you got everything?

ANNIE: 'Course I bloody have; I had to drag it off her at the end; she's sitting up there, with her fist stuck in her mouth. Cow. (Waits for NICK to take the bundles.)

NICK: I'll not touch it, fetch it down.

ANNIE tosses the cloth bundle to him.

NICK catches it.

NICK: It's wick; oh my God I felt it move, I felt it move mother, it's still bloody wick...

ANNIE grabs the bundle back and throws it down into the cellar, and the newspaper parcel after it.

ANNIE: You get it under that flagstone; it'll not move then.

She shoves him down the steps.

ANNIE: It's yours, you deal with it. (Shuts the door on him and leans against it, spent.)

MRS MATHER: You couldn't get him to kill a chicken at home; he's soft-hearted; it's hard on him, this. I know he's as much at fault as anyone Annie, I don't need you to point that out to me, even if he is my own son; but you have to pity him. He was frightened Annie, did you see? Thoroughly frightened. He'd no choice though.

When you think how often a woman'll pray to heaven to be

blessed with offspring, and they have none. . or they're not right that's born, or they don't live; the minister's wife at our chapel, just one such, and not a better living woman anywhere.

MRS MATHER opens the cellar door as ANNIE stands aside, and they look down.

NICK comes up, carrying the spade.

MRS MATHER: There now Nicky darling. Did you sweep away all the earth and all? There's a broom at the bottom of the steps just.

NICK: No.

MRS MATHER: You must.

NICK: I can't, it's still wick; I can't go back down there.

ANNIE: Just you come here a minute.

NICK (raises the spade): You keep away from me you. Get out of here. I'll bloody well kill you.

MRS MATHER clings to NICK, who, beside himself, waves the spade violently.

NICK: I swear I'll kill you! I'll kill the both of you!

MRS MATHER: Take no notice Annie love, it's his nerves, he's frightened out of his senses; they're soft, men; don't have what we have; he'll be right shortly.

NICK: D'you appreciate what you've made me do? Do you? It's under the flagstone, and when I replaced the flagstone . . did you <u>hear</u> it? It's little whimper? The squelch of it under me? Did you? D'you know what you've done to me? It's alive, it's really still alive. (Goes back to listen at the cellar door.) It's whimpering, you can hear it, listen, it's whimpering.

ANNIE (still shocked and shaken by his previous violence): That's all you can do isn't it, violence? Animal.

MRS MATHER: See he's going to finish it in a minute, never fret.

NICK: No it's quiet, I must have imagined it. Oh my God did you hear its soft little bones squelch? D'you appreciate what you've made me do? (Listens again.) It's whimpering, I can hear it, it's whimpering, really, how can it? Mum,

mum..

MRS MATHER: Take a moment Nick, there there love.

NICK: Mum I can't do anymore really I can't; have some pity for me.

MRS MATHER: Look at the state of you; here darling, somebody's left this whiskey out here: have that and perhaps you'll feel a bit better in yourself. (MR WHITEHEAD's whiskey.)

NICK (blubs): Mum, I feel as if I've reached the absolute limit, I can't go on from there, everything inside me's gone dead; I can't; its little bones squelched, and it whimpered mum, I heard it. D'you appreciate what you've made me do? I don't think you appreciate it at all. (Takes the offered whiskey.)

MRS MATHER: That's right, you have that, you need it. It's the dead hour now, you're bound to feel it, but you see, wait till that phone's ringing and the cars are going in and out, and people phoning and radio-ing in. New days come and go, and you'll forget even to think of it. (Goes off down the cellar steps.) Don't you worry about the tidying up, I'll see to that, never fear.

NICK gulps the whiskey, watches his mother go. Moves towards the house door.

NICK: I wonder if there's any more of that whiskey left by now? I could just do another.

The phone rings. ANNIE answers it.

ANNIE (on the phone): Mather's Taxis. (Jots the message.) Yes, that'll be all right, Botanical Road entrance? Right. Ten-thirty. Thank you. (Hangs up.)

NICK reappears in the doorway, he's found the bottle and is filling his tumbler.

ANNIE regards him.

ANNIE: Well? Your mother had it to do in the end I noticed. You've fancied yourself haven't you these last two years? My word you have; how does it feel now? Perhaps this'll take some of the gas out of you.

NICK walks to the cellar door.

NICK (at the cellar door, mutters): Mum, mum.

No reply.

NICK: Mum, pull the flagstone up, pull it up again, it's alive still; can't you hear it Annie? (Listens.) There: quite plain.

NICK has to move back as his mother pushes the door open.

NICK: It's whimpering.

MRS MATHER: Ouf! What's that Nicky lad? Everything's all right now, all tidy. Ouf, they're hard, those steps.

NICK: I can hear it, can't you?

MRS MATHER: Now there's nothing to hear Nicky darling, set your mind at rest.

NICK: What is that then? (Hands over his ears.) It's still whimpering, I'm sure it is; what am I going to do now. I can still hear it.

The phone rings, ANNIE answers it, jotting down the message.

ANNIE: Mather's Taxis, yes, yes, that's all right.

NICK (meanwhile): D'you appreciate what you've made me do? There's absolutely nowhere I can turn. (He goes into the house, cradling the whiskey to him.)

The SINGER comes on, as ANNIE finishes the call and she and MRS MATHER clear and the mirrored ball begins to turn.

SINGER (sings): The hardest thing in this world ever
The hardest thing in this world ever
The hardest thing in this world ever..
To have a trouble 'n no one to tell it to.

What's that stone you're carrying brother?
What's that stone you're carrying brother?
What's that stone you're carrying brother?
This stone's my trouble can I sell it to you?

I've got troubles wholesale feller
I've got troubles wholesale feller
I've got troubles wholesale feller
I can give twenty per cent discount to you.

The SINGER retires.

MICHAEL enters and seats himself, giggling tiredly, behind the table. His head sags.

AGNES enters.

AGNES (to us): Six weeks later; a weekday. Our Marion's getting married at last. She's not been so well, but she's all right now she reckons. (Indicates MICHAEL.) He's supposed to be driving people to the Registry Office, but look at him; drunk. Of all the days to pick. He's said he'd give Nick a day's driving for nothing, and see the state he's in.

MARIE comes in from the street, carrying shopping.

MARIE: Hallo.

AGNES: Hallo Marie.

MARIE: It's Marion's wedding then.

AGNES: Just look at the state of Michael there; he's drunk already, and he's said he'd do the driving. Some hopes.

MARIE: Would you do me a favour and get my old man to come out here to me? You know the people in there, and they'll be mostly strangers to me.

AGNES: I think they could've invited you Marie; your Mathew's the groom's relation isn't he?

MARIE: Yes, he's his nephew, but we've a lot on just now.

AGNES: I like weddings.

MARIE: Mathew just came by to wish them luck and I said I'd call for him here; so could you tell him I'm here and I've a load of shopping and can he come now?

AGNES (goes): All right.

MARIE (to us): Two years since I was here; crying for Nicky. I'd liked to have seen him... don't know why, to see how he is with Annie really I suppose. Silly really. I'll have been in his mind, but he didn't want to work all his life, it had to be Annie. Oh my God he hurt me.

NICK appears in the house doorway, in shirt sleeves, without a tie.

NICK: Marie!

MARIE: You knew I was here.

NICK: I didn't.

MARIE: Yes you did, Agnes told you.

NICK: No. No she didn't.

MARIE: How are you?

NICK: What you doing out here?

MARIE: I only came for Mathew, I've been shopping.

NICK: You should have come for the reception, you could have had a laugh at me.

MARIE: Why should I want to laugh at anybody? What's to laugh at?

NICK: Plenty to laugh at, considering what passed between you and me once.

MARIE: That's over a long time. I came for my husband; he's in there isn't he?

NICK: Not even a kiss for old time's sake? Not even for friendliness.

MARIE: There's no reason to.

NICK: No there isn't is there? If a dog comes fawning for a pat there's no reason to give it a pat is there?

MARIE: You wouldn't stop at a pat.

NICK: That's right, I wouldn't would I, bad dog. I feel awful Marie; I couldn't stay in there, I felt that bad; I wish I could just shut my eyes and it'd all go away; I couldn't bear to look at them in there, honestly, I had to vacate the room.

MARIE: Whatever have they done?

NICK: Mm? It's this thing I have on my mind, it's always on my mind, I can't stop it; and nothing, not drink nor sleep or anything, nothing whatever'll take it away; I feel as if I were very seriously ill, only in my heart, in my mind Marie; I don't mean I'm daft or anything like that: sick. And what's worse, what makes it hardest to bear: I can't tell anyone what it is. So don't ask me.

MARIE: You're not the only one that's had a hard time Nicky; I've had a hard time too, remember? I came through it.

NICK: Oh I know, I know it, and I apologize for it; but that was something you could come through; but I can't come through this, there's no end to this, I've nowhere to turn d'you see? And there's no end to it.

MARIE: And yet you've got so much.

NICK: No no, I may have certain things, but I'm sick at heart Marie; if only you'd known how to hold onto me, if only I hadn't gotten into this mess. It's no good, the way I'm living Marie, I shouldn't be separated from you.

MARIE: Mathew knows about you and me Nicky, and he doesn't hold it against me, and I'm thankful for what he's done for me; he sees me right, and I've no complaints. You've got what you wanted, so don't you complain either.

NICK: Me? Look Marie, it's a wedding, you don't have to tell me that, so I shan't spoil everything, but I'm not kidding, I could take the key of one of the cars from the drawer, get out onto the moors, and pile up into some handy wall; that's how things are with me Marie.

MARIE: Don't talk like that.

NICK: I'm not drunk you know; by no means; I couldn't get drunk today, no matter how much I was to drink; there's no pleasure whatsoever for me anymore. I've no one and nowhere to turn to, I'm not kidding.

MARIE: What about Annie? Who else should you turn to but your own wife? Leave other men's wives alone, you must have loved her once over, turn to her again.

NICK: I never meant anything wrong just then with you Marie, I'm sorry; I'm sick at heart and that's an end to it.

MARIE: I'm going to find Mathew. . (Exit. )

NICK buries his face in his hands.

AGNES: Dad, Dad, what you standing there for with your head in your hands? Everybody's waiting.

NICK: There's absolutely no way out for me, no way to turn whatever.

AGNES: You what? did you speak?

NICK remains tranced, sullen and silent.

AGNES: Dad, come on, get ready for the wedding, please, you'll spoil everything.

NICK: Oh get off.

AGNES (takes his arm): You'll have them wondering what's wrong.

NICK drags himself loose and turns on her, muddled and angry.

NICK: You get off it Agnes, d'you hear me? Leave this room at once!

AGNES: I'll get our Mam to you. (Exit.)

NICK: I absolutely refuse to go in there; I simply couldn't. Not look at Marion, not stand there smiling at them all, I'd rather do anything than that. There's one solution, that I do know. Absolute peace at ninety miles an hour. (He reaches over to the table drawer and roots in it. The key he wants is not there, he rejects a couple after examination. He considers the torpid MICHAEL, goes round the table and is rooting cautiously in MICHAEL's pocket as his mother enters hurriedly; NICK drags his hand out hastily.)

MRS MATHER: Now then Nicky darling, everyone's waiting, and you without your coat and tie; come along with you love.

NICK: It was your doing; I am no longer a man.

MRS MATHER: Now whatever kind of talk is that? Of course you're a man don't talk such nonsense; you've got to give the bride away, so hurry up.

NICK: Ha!

MRS MATHER: That's a very curious reaction; are you worried you won't know how to go on?

NICK: Are you aware of the relations I've had with Marion? D'you consider that at all?

MRS MATHER: I'm sure I'm very glad the way things have turned out, and that's all that matters; you'd better watch just what you're saying Nicholas Mather, or you'll come out with something we shall all regret. Marion's consented to marry of her own free will, and if that's what she wants I'm sure it's no business of ours to stand in the way of her happiness.

NICK: Her own free will my foot.

MRS MATHER: She's marrying of her own free will; she'll be in a bigger mess if she doesn't, so she chooses to marry. If she'd behaved properly in the first instance, none of this need have happened, so she's only herself to blame.

There's nothing whatever wrong with young Geoffrey, and he came courting her in the first place; he fell off a bit I know, but I was able to put her in his way again and he didn't raise any great objections that I noticed; and you've been more than generous in seeing them set up in married life; there's not a hair out of place Nicholas darling.

NICK: I should be extremely interested to know how you feel about that thing in the cellar that's all; I mean you do consider that?

MRS MATHER: I'm sure we don't know what you're talking about; really Nicholas, you're extremely odd in your behaviour sometimes, I shall just ignore you.

NICK: It's on my mind all the time, the noise Mother... the noise its little bones made.. You stand there and pretend it's not happened, you just stand there..

MRS MATHER: Now just listen to me Nicholas Mather and this is for the last time; you get back in there and you just get your coat and tie on; people are beginning to talk, among themselves; if they start to put two and two together, and they see you dragging your feet, you will be in trouble. So let's have no more of this moaning; you get in there my lad.

NICK: No no, I can't do it, no no no..

ANNIE comes in, blowsy in her best clothes, rosy with drink, her eyes swimming, and her hair only just in place.

ANNIE: Now then Mrs Mather, we're all set; where's Nicky?

MRS MATHER: Look at him, ooh he is obstinate my lad, he won't shift.

ANNIE wobbles genteelly over for a look at NICK.

NICK (mutters evasively, beside himself): Is that really what I've to live with? You make me sick, are you aware of that?

ANNIE: You've been having too much to drink darling? You ought to have a lay down for ten minutes, I'll come with you. No, no, don't be naughty; come on now Nicky, you lean on me'n come'n see everybody. I've set the record player on, and everybody's very pleased with the arrangements. Where've you been darling? Out here on your own? It's been very nice.

NICK: What's nice?

ANNIE: The arrangements, I told you, and all the presents, and everything. We've been looking at the cake. Come on.

NICK: You go in, I'll be along in a minute.

ANNIE: Don't be cross Nicky love, everything'll be different when she's gone and settled, it'll be lovely, you see. We'll be happy together, like we were once. I'm so happy, don't spoil things by being silly Nicky, please; it's as if it were my own wedding again, such kindness, such lovely people ... oh they are pleased.

NICK: So why didn't you stay in there with them?

ANNIE: No, no Nicky don't please. I've had a lot of trouble and pain, and it's over now. You come on and get your coat and tie, and we can all set off for the Registry Office.

NICK: <u>Yes</u>, all <u>right</u>, I will; just give me a moment, for heaven's sake; there's absolutely no kind of privacy. I said I'm coming.

MRS MATHER: Come on then Annie love, he's promised you, and he won't go back on that I know.

The two women go into the house.

NICK (to us): I wasn't lying when I said that either; I'm coming, oh yes. And I won't be a moment before I'm gone, no lies. My God did you see the sight of her? she won't fancy me so well when they find my body.

He sets himself to extract the key from whichever pocket MICHAEL has it in.
After drawing a couple of blanks, during which MICHAEL's drugged eyes open and his poor old eyes swivel into focus, NICK lights on a key and draws it out.
He examines it to make sure it's the right one.
MICHAEL opens his eyes fully, and brings his strong hand down on NICK's, gripping key and hand together.

MICHAEL: Ah-ha, you don't drive today Mr Mather, oh no. I made you a promise; you have your fun today, drink what you like, I'm the driver, and it won't cost you a penny; wedding present, that.

NICK: Let me have the key.

MICHAEL: You're not listening, are you? It's the boss isn't it? Thought it was. I'll just show you something, boss.

MICHAEL cups his other hand under the one gripping NICK, and concentrates as he squeezes the gripped hand as if getting juice from a lemon.

NICK darts out his other hand to the rescue of the gripped one, and then draws it back as it seems to bring on more, not less, pain.

MICHAEL loosens his grip, and pokes out the key from NICK's hand.

MICHAEL: Sorry boss.

NICK: Give me that key.

MICHAEL: No no no no, I said I'd drive today see. (Rises, slides to the floor, hoists himself up again to the chair.) Whiskey's got to my legs, but I'm still a good driver boss! you try me! better than ever when I've had a few!

NICK: Give me that flaming key you drunken bloody waster! Give it to me! give it me give it me give it me you bastard give it me! (He weeps with enraged frustration.)

MICHAEL: I'm very fond of you boss, but you're stupid; stewpid. You're frightened aren't you? Frightened to face 'em out eh? What Can They Do To You that's worse'n What You're Doing To Yourself Eh? Answer me that? Look at me: frightened of nobody; you don't frighten me, nobody frightens me; I don't depend on you, you don't depend on me, nobody depends on me nobody.
'I'm a poor little lamb who has lost his way
Baa baa..'
I went teetotal didn't I? And see what happens. Drunk again. You don't frighten me you know, nobody frightens me; when I drink I drink. It's like a whirling hurricane of madness, a HUGE nightmare blowing up inside me, 'n all the time this face here is hanging on the front, grinning and dribbling and drinking and wondering what's going on out there that could be WORSE than what's going on inside. I'll be on the blind for bloody WEEKS I will! celebration, you watch me go. I'll sell cap, coat, jacket, trousers, boots. Nobody frightens me. I ended up in the Glasshouse I did, when I was a soldier, account of my drinking. Kicked the living shite out of me; that'll teach you to drink they said; that's what you bloody think I said: I was bloody parched.
Not afraid of them, what could a SCREW do to me? It was all done already, HA!

A Padre once says to me he says 'The devil's a braggart', he says, 'and braggarts have no guts.' Too bloody right I says, shun the devil and stick to strong drink, 'cause I know that cowardice is a sin, and strong drink is as brave as a lion. Let yourself down in front of people, that's hell that is. And that's why I have a good life of it: sod 'em all I say.

NICK: I've been a fool to myself.

MICHAEL: Mm?

NICK: I've been a fool to myself.

MICHAEL: Oh so have I, so have I. Still and all there's nothing to be afraid of in that: don't let 'em bother you, they're all some mother's son, all the same height when they're on their backs. Have a drink of this.

MICHAEL produces a small bottle of whiskey, offers it.

NICK swallows it.

MICHAEL: Oh hell, that's the bloody lot boss that is.

MRS MATHER hurries in followed by ANNIE carrying NICK's coat and tie, and then followed by the rest of the guests.

MRS MATHER: Ah, there you are Nicholas, we're all ready now.

ANNIE: Get your coat and tie on darling, everybody's ready.

NICK: I absolutely refuse to live a life of lies any more! I completely reject it.

MRS MATHER: Yes dear? What's that you say?

ANNIE: Come on everyone! he's just getting his coat on! What a fuss eh? Anyone'd think it was us getting married not Marion and Geoffrey! (To NICK:) Give us five minutes to get started, then you follow on with Marion and with Michael driving.

NICK: Dad, have you a minute?

MRS MATHER: What's that son? There isn't a lot of time.. we're due at the Registry Office Nick, you know that?

The GUESTS crowd out, the ball turns.

NICK: I could do with your help a minute Dad. Could I have everybody's attention please? Could you all wait a minute please.

GUEST: He's going to make a speech.

NICK: One moment please everybody; leave off Annie, d'you mind?

ANNIE struggles to get him into his jacket and tie.

NICK: Marion! could you just come in here please?

SECOND GUEST: What is it Mr Mather? Marion shouldn't be out here now, she'll see the groom, oh dear; I just wish you'd inform someone what's going on; we shall be late at the Registry Office, and you know how they don't like it.

NICK: Dad, listen please, if you will, I've a piece of information for you all..

A POLICEMAN appears in the street door.

POLICEMAN: Excuse me! These cars outside; excuse me! these cars outside! you can't have 'em waiting out here for ever you know. Are you all coming out to them or not?

NICHOLAS goes to confront the GUESTS and attempts to kneel before them.

MR & MRS MATHER, ANNIE & AGNES, hurry forward to haul him to his feet and prevent such a scene.

AGNES: Have your legs gone? (To us:) His legs have gone on him.

ANNIE: Nicholas what is it?

AGNES: It's his legs mam, hold him up.

MR MATHER: What d'you mean his legs? What's wrong with his legs?

NICK: Let me kneel! I want to kneel! here, in front of everyone.

AGNES: He says he wants to kneel.

NICK: I imagine I can kneel if I want to!

GUEST: He's drunk I bet.

POLICEMAN: Is that you there Mr Mather? D'you hear what I'm saying?

MRS MATHER: For heaven's sake pull yourself together; what's got into you?

MATHER: He's like rubber.

NICK: Friends! Neighbours! I should just like you to hear me out, if you please, I've got something of importance to say!

MRS MATHER (hauling him up): Have you gone raving mad? I'm sorry everybody, I don't know what you must think, I don't know what's the matter with him I truly don't; he's been very bad with his nerves recently, that's all I know. I think we'd better get him into the house for a minute.

POLICEMAN: Is he ill?

NICK: Get your hands off me!!

MARION appears at the house door, stopping efforts to get NICK through into the back out of the way.

NICK swings in the grip of his family to face the company. The GUESTS chat, embarrassedly.

MICHAEL: You give it to 'em Nicky boy! (Sings cheerfully.) 'We are poor little lambs..'

NICK: Marie, I did the wrong thing by you, I let you down; I promised you I'd marry you, and you trusted me, and I knew you had no one else to turn to, and I betrayed you that trust: I took you, and I told you extremely untruthful lies, and then I simply cast you aside.

MICHAEL: 'Doomed from here to eternity...'

NICK: Sharrap Michael!!! For Christ's sake this is serious! I'm sorry, I'm sorry everybody, I apologize.

MRS MATHER (weeping with weariness and humiliation): Please Nicky, don't do this, please...

NICK: Well let me kneel! I want to kneel!

MRS MATHER: No no Nicky please..

NICK: Marion, Marion, I've done the wrong thing by you; your father didn't die a natural death; he was given pills and they gradually weakened him by taking away his appetite until he wasted away completely... Because of my clandestine affair with your mother this happened.

ANNIE: Now that's enough, Nicky, I say it's <u>enough</u>!!

POLICEMAN: Excuse me. (Goes to the phone.) I'll use your phone if I may.

MATHER: He wants to kneel, let him kneel; and you rozzer, listen to what he says.

POLICEMAN: I'm sorry sir, but I must contact the station. .

MATHER: If that isn't typical of the Police.

The mirror ball begins to turn.

NICK: Marion! I took your father from you, and I followed that up by taking everything you'd got away from you; I seduced you into my bed, your own stepfather, I put you where my lawful wife should have been, out of common lust.
I brought about your father's demise.
I spoiled your life for you, ruined your chances.
I seduced you into my bed where your mother should have been.
And I killed the baby.
Our baby.
My baby.
I took the life of a newborn child.
I lifted up a flagstone in the cellar of this house.
I scraped away the earth underneath with a trenching tool.
I laid the baby in the shallow hole which I'd made.
I laid the flagstone back over it.
And.
And.
And.
I stood on the flagstone, to force it back into place neatly.
And its bones and its body.
And its bones and its body.
Squelched under my weight.

MRS MATHER and ANNIE let him go and he folds humbly to the floor AGNES holding one arm.

POLICEMAN: All right, that's enough Mr Mather, you'll have to accompany me to the station and make a statement; come along everybody, let's have this room cleared if you please, there'll be no wedding today. I shall want all of your names . . . if you'll just give them to me, together with your addresses, as you leave. I'm assuming you've got corroboration of all this Mr Mather?

MARION: Yes.

All the GUESTS leave, pausing to give names and addresses to the POLICEMAN. The FAMILY go into the house. Finally the POLICEMAN helps NICK out of the office.

THE END

## Songs from the Play (Tunes: Alex Glasgow)

THIS JOCKEY DRIVES LATE NIGHTS (p7, p46)

3.
Bmi
Oh that tinkling key that jails me Takes away
my days stoned out
F#
Cat's eyes snake on
sparks-from-the-big-knife-grinder
4.
Bmi
Man at the wheel says nothing Locked up in thunder
F#
this man
Clock don't go from way
back gave up
5.
Bmi
Two matchsticks hold my lids up Boys like the
mouse in the wheel he
F#
says One day I'il reach the end of
this long journey
ENDING :-
shadow of a running
F#
man
Bmi

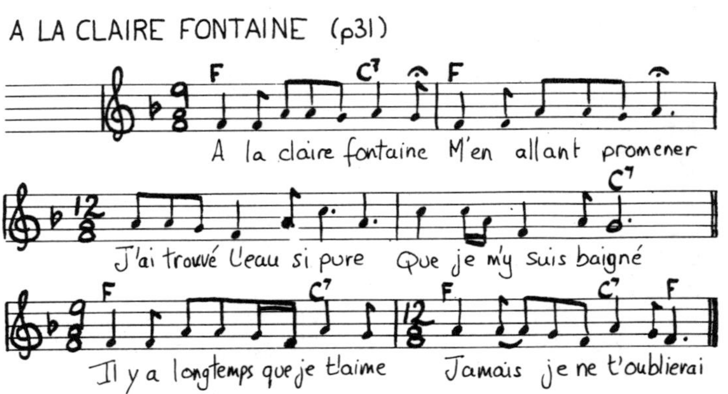
A LA CLAIRE FONTAINE (p31)
F C7 F
A la claire fontaine M'en allant promener
C7
J'ai trouvé l'eau si pure Que je m'y suis baigné
F C7 F C7 F
Il y a longtemps que je t'aime Jamais je ne t'oublierai

OH TAKE THE LEAP (p67)
A B
In one block of flats lived Syd's friend Alice And
E A B
our Syd lived with us The flats is high the lifts was bust So they
E A Bmi
courted at long distances Oh take the leap oh take the plunge Shun
E7 A
not the joys of marriage
N.B. V.2,3,4,5 begin:- etc.

THE HARDEST THING IN THIS WORLD EVER (p80)
FREELY
Bmi
The hardest thing in this world ever The
F#
Bmi
hardest thing in this world ever The hardest thing in this
F#
Bmi
world ever To have a trouble 'n no one to tell it to
TEMPO
Bmi
F#
What's that stone you're carrying brother What's that stone you're
Bmi
carrying brother What's that stone you're carrying brother
F#
Bmi
This stone's my trouble can I sell it to you
V3 ends:
F#
Bmi
I can give twenty per cent discount to you

## Other Methuen Playscripts

| | |
|---|---|
| Paul Ableman | TESTS |
| | BLUE COMEDY |
| Barry Bermange | NATHAN AND TABILETH and OLDENBERG |
| John Bowen | THE CORSICAN BROTHERS |
| Howard Brenton | REVENGE |
| | CHRISTIE IN LOVE and OTHER PLAYS |
| | PLAYS FOR PUBLIC PLACES |
| Henry Chapman | YOU WON'T ALWAYS BE ON TOP |
| Peter Cheeseman | THE KNOTTY |
| David Cregan | THREE MEN FOR COLVERTON |
| | TRANSCENDING and THE DANCERS |
| | THE HOUSES BY THE GREEN |
| | MINIATURES |
| Rosalyn Drexler | THE INVESTIGATION and HOT BUTTERED ROLL |
| Simon Gray | THE IDIOT |
| John McGrath | EVENTS WHILE GUARDING THE BOFORS GUN |
| David Mercer | THE GOVERNOR'S LADY |
| Georges Michel | THE SUNDAY WALK |
| Rodney Milgate | A REFINED LOOK AT EXISTENCE |
| Guillaume Oyono-Mbia | THREE SUITORS: ONE HUSBAND and UNTIL FURTHER NOTICE |
| Alan Plater | CLOSE THE COALHOUSE DOOR |
| David Selbourne | THE PLAY OF WILLIAM COOPER AND EDMUND DEW-NEVETT |
| | THE TWO-BACKED BEAST |
| | DORABELLA |
| Wole Soyinka | CAMWOOD ON THE LEAVES |
| Johnny Speight | IF THERE WEREN'T ANY BLACKS YOU'D HAVE TO INVENT THEM |
| Martin Sperr | TALES FROM LANDSHUT |
| Boris Vian | THE KNACKER'S ABC |
| Lanford Wilson | HOME FREE! and THE MADNESS OF LADY BRIGHT |
| Harrison, Melfi, Howard | NEW SHORT PLAYS: 1 |
| Duffy, Harrison, Owens | NEW SHORT PLAYS: 2 |
| Barker, Grillo, Haworth, Simmons | NEW SHORT PLAYS: 3 |